GETTING
FREE
PUBLICITY

If you want to know how...

Marketing for Complementary Therapists
101 tried and tested ways to attract clients

100 Ways to Make Your Busines a Success
A resource book for small businesses

Save £1000s Selling Your Home
Learn an estate agent's secrets and make more money

**Producing Successful Magazines,
Newsletters and E-Zines**

170101

GETTING FREE PUBLICITY

The secrets

of successful

press relations

Pam & Bob Austin

howtobooks

Published by How To Books Ltd,
3 Newtec Place, Magdalen Road,
Oxford OX4 1RE. United Kingdom.
Tel: (01865) 793806. Fax: (01865) 248780.
email: info@howtobooks.co.uk
http://www.howtobooks.co.uk

British Library Cataloguing in Publication Data
A catalogue record for this book is available from the British
Library

Cover design by Baseline Arts Ltd, Oxford
Produced for How To Books by Deer Park Productions,
Tavistock
Typeset by PDQ Typesetting, Newcastle-under-Lyme, Staffs.
Printed and bound by Cromwell Press, Trowbridge, Wiltshire

NOTE: The material contained in this book is set out in good
faith for general guidance and no liability can be accepted
for loss or expense incurred as a result of relying in particular
circumstances on statements made in the book. The laws and
regulations are complex and liable to change, and readers should
check the current position with the relevant authorities before
making personal arrangements.

Contents

Introduction

'Is there something here that's **new, free or amazing**?' That's how journalists often judge news stories. This book, which is all about promoting your business or organisation in the press, is certainly **new**. The book's not **free** – but it will certainly help you to get free publicity! And as you read it, you'll find it **amazing** how easy it is to succeed at press relations, once you get to know the territory and the language.

A quarter of a century working in press relations – and spending much of that time working with relatively small, owner-managed business clients – has taught us three basic Facts of Life. Here they are:

- Most businesses like the idea of regular publicity in their trade magazines.
- Many believe that they can't afford professional press relations.
- Some get the feeling that they ought to be able to do PR themselves.

If you identify with one or more of these Facts of Life, this DIY manual of press relations practice has been written specially for you. It takes you step by step from the basics of 'Why press relations?', what makes journalists tick, ways of choosing and presenting stories to give them the best chance of acceptance by editors, through to what happens if your lovely relationship goes pear-shaped.

You're already involved with a PR agency? *Getting Free Publicity* will help you to understand what your agency's trying to do for you, and why – it will put you both on the same wavelength. And if you're thinking of taking the DIY route to fame and fortune in the press, you couldn't choose a more experienced travelling companion.

We hope you will profit by it – and enjoy it!

Pam and Bob Austin

Getting Noticed by Your Customers

Today there are lots of ways in which you can put your name, products and services in front of your prospective customers – personal sales calls, telesales, direct mail and email, websites, exhibitions, TV advertising, press advertising, editorial mentions. Which to use is a marketing decision depending on many factors, and there are negative as well as positive considerations. For example, business people and householders alike are becoming increasingly irritated with a rising tide of junk snail-mail, spam e-mails, Tracy or Kevin from the telephone call centre, and unscheduled reps' visits 'just to make sure we're looking after you alright'.

However, it does seem that the pages of the trade and consumer press are still keeping their popularity as a promotional medium. When the latest issue of *Widgets International* or *Today's Gardener* pops through the door or lands on the desk, there's often a feeling that 'my' magazine has arrived. Many are read from cover to cover with genuine interest and respect, and often in quiet moments when the reader has time to absorb the contents.

So there you are, relaxed, coffee to hand and gently turning the pages of your favourite industry mag, when...DAMN! *It's happened again!* Your major competitor has once again got his name in there with a good, positive news story which is now being read with interest by thousands of your prospective buyers. *Why on earth aren't we in there?*

The answer is simple – you should be, you could be, *but you're not trying to be.* Question: How do we go about trying to get in there? What's most effective – advertising, or editorial? And is it worthwhile anyway?

THE BASICS
Let's start from Square One. There are just two ways of getting your company's name to appear in the press, and you could use one or both:

- by aiming for free coverage in the **editorial** pages
- by buying **advertising** space.

Editorial
Editorial items that appear in magazines – articles, case studies, news stories – are largely written and submitted by press relations agencies or in-house PR professionals.

Readers may be subconsciously aware of this when they are reading them. Even so, they feel that the companies, products or services that are mentioned somehow carry the independent endorsement of the magazine. Also readers will often relate to, for example, a case study describing a problem that arose and how it was solved with a particular product or service – 'we've got a problem like that'.

Advertising

Advertising, on the other hand, while it can certainly make an impact, also prompts a feeling of 'they've had to pay money to say that' – and, of course, they have. The level of price will depend upon the publication's standing in the industry and its distribution, and will be based on space (full page, half-page, etc.) for a display ad or, for classified ads, lineage or column inches/centimetres. Add to this the cost of good, professional artwork; unless you have a fairly hefty promotional budget, the same artwork tends to get used in the same publications month after month after month. This may be good economics, but it's also dead boring.

Advertorial

Worthy of mention here is the so-called 'advertorial'. This consists of one or more pages that look just like editorial pages, but are actually paid advertising. Look carefully, and you will find the words 'advertising feature' or something similar, probably in quite small type at the top of each page. Advertorials can be expensive because of the space they occupy, but you might occasionally be offered a bargain by an advertisement manager who is trying to hit his sales target.

Pros and cons

Advertisements and advertorials do have one thing going for them. Because you pay for them, you call the shots. If space is available, they will be published as, when and how you want them to be. This is something that cannot be guaranteed with news stories and other copy that you send to editors. You don't have to pay for editorial material to appear (unless you fall for the magazine's request for so-called colour separation charges to use any pictures you send with them), but usage is entirely at the editor's discretion (see the next chapter).

However, it is worth pressing on with the editorial route because surveys over the years have shown that readers are invariably influenced more by what they read in the editorial pages than by advertisements. Editorial mentions result in more and higher quality enquiries than advertisements produce. Also, the cost of achieving the editorial mention may be only a fraction of the cost of buying advertising space.

EDITORIAL VERSUS ADVERTISING – SOME FACTS AND FIGURES

Some years ago, one of our SME (Small/Medium-sized Enterprise) clients carried out its own survey. The client, a company marketing water treatment products, had launched a new device – we'll call it 'Xproduct' – that prevented the build-up of limescale in domestic and industrial water installations. We promoted Xproduct through the editorial pages of the press by writing and placing a series of news stories, technically-oriented articles and case studies. At the same time, the client also placed regular paid advertisements in trade magazines and kept a careful analysis of all incoming enquiries from both sources.

During the first 12 months, we wrote six editorial articles and placed them with plumbing and building maintenance magazines. We also wrote and distributed nine news releases covering orders and installations, new additions to the Xproduct range, and so on. In months 10, 11 and 12 of the campaign, the client placed five paid advertisements. In the same period Xproduct also had six editorial mentions resulting from our activities.

The five advertisements produced 235 enquiries – average, 47 per advertisement. Yet the six editorial mentions produced 414 enquiries – an average of 69 per mention, and *46 per cent more than advertising.*

In one month it so happened that a half-page advertisement and an editorial article of about 1,000 words appeared in the same issue of one magazine. This conjunction was not planned; however, it did give the client an opportunity to make a direct comparison of the relative impact made by each item. The half-page advertisement produced 133 enquiries, the editorial produced 172 – *30 per cent more.* Cost-wise, *the client had paid seven times more* for the half-page advertisement than we had charged them for writing and placing the 1,000 word article. So it was hardly surprising that the client commented that 'the results, in terms of enquiries and new business, have been both impressive and cost-effective'.

Assuming that you've decided to go down the editorial route, you will be moving into unknown territory – the mysterious world of journalists and editors. Indeed, the media relations business has been described as 'attempting to control an uncontrollable activity'. Yet once you discover what goes on in the editorial jungle, how it works and what makes its inhabitants tick, you should get on just fine.

Making Your Mark with Journalists

For most wannabe spin-doctors, establishing good relationships with editors and journalists will **not** involve alcoholic lunches, expensive Christmas presents and other freebies. The list of publications relevant to your products and services could run into dozens – maybe hundreds. You may only actually meet a handful of journalists face to face; the editorial staff of many industrial and trade mags consists of the editor, and maybe a half share in a PA. Good heavens! They could be even busier than you are! You may speak to some of them on the phone occasionally, but much of your contact with the press will be at a distance.

By the way, gentlemen, a timely warning for the more macho among you. Lots of journalists and editors are women. Journalism is a profession in which men and women really do compete as equals – check the by-lines in any newspaper. So if someone called Caroline or Tamara phones to check something in one of your recent press releases, don't make the fatal mistake of treating her as if she's the Editor's Little Helper. *She could well be the editor...*

And we hope that all women journos will forgive us if, in these pages, we use the word 'he' as shorthand for 'he/she' when referring to members of the Fourth Estate.

LIFE ON PLANET JOURNO

Face to face or at arm's length, your PR success or otherwise will rely heavily upon:

♦ your understanding of how the press works

♦ knowing what journalists/editors want (and don't want!)

♦ how to present it to them in ways that make their lives as easy as possible.

> **Fact: When you can adjust to, and accept, the way that editors and journalists think and work, you will be a long way down the road to successful press relations.**

Here are some pointers.

GIVE THEM *STORIES*

You probably judge your own business success by the level of sales or profit you or your company achieves. *Journalists look at life differently*. Editors may take a keen interest in their magazine's circulation figures, but the average journalist's career revolves around **stories**. There's an old but true saying that a journalist is only as good as his last front-page story. 'What the hell's the *story*?' is a frustrated cry all too often heard from an editor – and usually just before he consigns a press release to the bin.

Once you understand this elementary fact about journalists, it becomes obvious that you will make friends with them not by giving them lunches, but by giving them **stories**. And a good story gives you an edge in the useability stakes, because some of the stuff that arrives on editors' desks is so awful that it can only be – and usually is! – described as 'crap copy' (there, now you've learned another term of the trade).

Example: A three-page single-spaced 'news release' setting out your chairman's views on the current state of the world economy (yes, it does happen!). Sending out the release may do great things for your chairman's ego. In practice it will be a total waste of time, paper and postage, make you look a rank amateur, and hit every editorial waste-bin in Fleet Street. Why? Because unless your company is a highly successful zillion-dollar multinational, *who gives a damn what your chairman thinks about the world economy?* That's right – **it's not a story**, and a true PR professional would have known that. You may score Brownie points with your chairman, but it's black marks all round from all those editors whose time you have wasted.

We discuss what makes good news stories, and how to tell them, in Chapter 5, but just one more point about stories at this stage. It's all too easy to fall into the trap of thinking that you haven't got any stories to tell. **You have**.

Once you've got this need for stories firmly fixed in your mind, you will (hopefully) start looking at everything your company does in terms of news stories. A high-value or interesting customer order, the development of a new and clever widget, the appointment of a new customer-facing executive or distributor, a move into new premises, showing at a trade exhibition – they're all potential news stories. And if you still claim that your organisation hasn't got any, maybe you should ask yourself why you are working for a bunch of no-hopers that sits there doing nothing.

BE VERY NICE TO THE EDITOR

The editor of any publication is a total autocrat. He, and he alone, has the final decision as to which stories, articles, etc. are used and which are not. Editors need these draconian powers, partly because they are solely responsible to the publisher for the readability and reputation of the publication, and partly because they can be personally sued for expensive things like libel (see Chapter 11).

Knowing this may help to ease the frustration if, as sometimes happens, an editor doesn't use the first couple of news stories you send him. If the editor doesn't know you, he may want to be sure that you're not one of those here-today-and-gone-tomorrow outfits before he puts your name in front of his readers. So he waits until he's seen a few of your press releases coming across his desk to convince him that you're real, interesting and here to stay. Simple, when you think about it!

To avoid incurring the imperial displeasure:

◆ *Don't* threaten to appeal to a higher authority if the editor doesn't use your story. *There is no higher authority to appeal to.*

◆ *Don't* try to pressure an editor to use your stories on the grounds that you advertise in his magazine. Most editors have little or nothing to do with advertising, and value their independence.

◆ *Don't* waste his time (and yours) by phoning and asking him if he'll be using the story you've just sent him. Read the next issue and you'll find out.

◆ *Don't* suggest that an editor really must use a particular story you've sent him because the industry has been waiting for it with bated breath, or that it's a matter of vital public interest. The editor will be the sole judge of that, thank you – just write it well, send it in, and say your prayers.

◆ *Don't* phone and ask an editor why he didn't use your last story. Non-appearance may be for any one of several reasons, but *he doesn't owe you an explanation* and may resent your implication that he does. So better not to ask at all, yes?

By now you may be feeling that establishing good relationships with such godlike beings is Mission Impossible. Take heart – most editors are quite human really. They actually rely on people like you to send them news stories, articles and case studies to fill the editorial pages of their magazines, although it would probably be very counter-productive to remind them of this!

Try to understand the imperatives and constraints on them, fit in with their needs, treat them with friendly respect as professionals in their field, and you'll get along just fine.

ALWAYS ASK: 'WHAT'S YOUR DEADLINE?'

Imagine, if you can, producing a monthly magazine. As a minimum you would have to allow time every month for getting all the news, articles, etc. sorted out, deciding what's going on which page, what pictures to use and, finally, getting the whole thing off to the printers in time for them to print it and get it to the distributors by the due date. To facilitate this, editors and journalists have to work to tight deadlines – and so must you. This affects you in two ways:

1. If a journalist phones and asks for some information which you don't have at your fingertips (or that you want to think about first), always ask: 'What's your deadline for this?' It may be the end of this week; it

may be the end of today. Whatever it is, honour it and you'll earn yourself Brownie points.

2. Quite a few monthly trade and industry magazines close for copy round about the middle of the month before publication, e.g. if you want to hit April issues you will probably need to get your copy to the editor by about 10th – 12th March. This is only a general rule of thumb, and news stories mostly take their chances. However, if you are submitting a feature article requested for a particular issue of a magazine, do make sure you know what the editor's copy deadline is. If he doesn't tell you, *ask him*.

WHATEVER HAPPENS, *DON'T LIE*

Telling lies is a sure and certain way to wreck a beautiful friendship with a journalist. All PR people put a touch of 'spin' on a story from time to time – maybe leaving out something which is better left unsaid (like, it's a wonderful piece of kit but maybe best not to mention its out-of-sight delivery time). But *never, never tell a direct lie to a journalist*, either verbally or in a written news story. If he accepts it as genuine and acts on it, and then it proves to be a lie, he will never trust you again. It's all part of the stories thing, it's about his professionalism. He needs to get a reputation for accuracy, for getting his stories right. You've broken the trust he placed in you, you've dented his reputation. He won't risk it next time.

$$\left(3 \right)$$

Getting Media Attention

There are certain tools you can use to create a positive image of your organisation in the press. Each has its own specific task. As a useful exercise, dig out one or two of your trade magazines and see if you can identify them. We'll go into more detail on each one later, but this is what your toolkit looks like:

THE Press reLations TOOLKIT

PRESS RELEASES

A variety of short news stories which combine over a period to build up a picture of an active and successful company – winning orders, developing new products and services, appointing new people, attending exhibitions, and so on.

Aim to send out at least one story every month because, almost without exception, **the success of any PR campaign will depend entirely on the quality and regularity of your press releases.** Until you have built up that positive, successful-company image in the minds of editors – and press releases are the only way of doing this – you will not get a chance to use the next two tools.

ARTICLES

Sometimes known as 'feature articles' because they are often written to fit in with a feature in a specific issue of a publication (see 'Features monitoring' below). They discuss subjects such as a current topic affecting a particular industry, or the pros and cons of a new technology. The aim here is to present the writer to the readership as the expert in the field – and hopefully as an industry guru to whom journalists will instinctively turn for comments as and when this subject arises again.

After your steady flow of well-written press releases has convinced the editor that you know your stuff, he may look favourably on an article written by one of your people, by-lined with his name, title, and your company's name. The editor may insist on a so-called 'generic' article, i.e. one which does not specifically plug your company or its products (but don't throw in the towel, there's a way of getting round this – see page 62).

CASE STUDIES

Case studies are articles that take an in-depth look at a particular situation or problem which arose, and describe how it was solved. Well documented case studies are popular with editors, and readers like them because they can often identify with them: 'Hey, we've got a problem like that'. They will be popular with you too, because you'll be able to splash out with the names of the products and services that were the key to the solution (yours, of course). Writing a generic case study is virtually impossible!

PHOTOGRAPHS

The impact of press releases, articles and case studies can be improved considerably by photographs (known in the biz as 'pics') – people, products, buildings, installed equipment.

One warning: if you are going to send pics, do make them directly relevant to the story. For instance, if your story is about a service agreement that a customer has signed with you, the only relevant pic would be one of the actual signing ceremony. If the best you can come up with is an aerial view of the customer's premises, probably better to forget it.

Pics must be sharp and clear, and not too small; a good size of print is 5″ x 7″. Take time and trouble to get good shots, and try to make them interesting and/or a little unusual – a mug-shot, to go with an appointment story, taken slightly to one side rather than the usual full-face passport job, perhaps. And do remember to caption your pictures to tell the editor what they are. This can be done with a short description printed on an adhesive label stuck to the back of the pic.

In this electronic age, editors often prefer to receive pictures by e-mail in the form of jpeg files. Hence, try to have high-resolution pics taken by digital camera or, if one isn't available, scan prints into your PC.

Getting hold of good pics might sound difficult, but there are usually ways round it. In your own organisation, it's possible that Marketing already has a library of product pics, and will know of a good local photographer who can take mug-shots for appointment stories. Pics involving third parties (equipment installed at a customer's premises, for example) can be trickier, especially if the customer is at some distance – you won't want the expense of sending your local photographer hundreds of miles across country to produce two shots of a widget-forming machine.

If the customer has a Press Office or a PR agency, try asking them if they have anything suitable. Look at the customer's website – maybe you could download something suitable from there? Alternatively, check with your customer to see if he would cooperate, then phone the nearest local newspaper office and speak to their photographer – many of them are freelances and may be prepared to take local shots for a reasonable fee, provided that someone is there on site to show them what to take. And if you're going to the site yourself to research a case study, and you're a bit of a dab hand with a camera, why not try taking a few yourself? Even if the quality's not quite up to David Bailey standards, modern digital enhancement technology can sometimes work wonders...

There is a tendency among many publications to contact you after you've sent them a photograph with a press release, asking if you will agree to pay so-called **colour separation charges**. These can range from around £85 to more than £200, and the (unsaid) implication is that if you don't pay, they won't use the release to which the pic relates. Some make good on the threat, some don't. What's it all about?

Until recently, printing a colour photograph called for the manufacture of separate printing plates in primary colours, and this generated platemaking costs. Today's computer-to-plate digital technology does not require colour separations but, strange as it may seem, many magazines don't seem to have noticed this! Refusing to pay, using a diplomatic excuse such as 'I'm afraid we don't have the budget for it', will not necessarily result in refusal to use the story. However, if a particular publication is a very important one in your marketplace and you can afford the fee they are asking, you may feel that it's a worthwhile investment to make sure your story and your beautiful pic get in there.

PRESS LISTS

Before starting an active press relations campaign, you have to decide on your target audience – who you are going to send your press releases to. You need to create a Press List.

Now it's Policy Decision Time, because there are two methods to choose from:

The sniper

Using this method, you select a limited number of targets in your sector and aim individual releases at them. You can select the targets by asking yourself which trade or professional publications are the most important in your sector, which ones you read regularly, and then ask your colleagues (and maybe some of your customers) the same question. A restricted list is relatively easy to handle; you can take and read all of the publications regularly to judge the effectiveness of your campaign, and maybe you can get close to the small handful of journalists involved.

The shotgun

There will be certain publications that directly serve your industry. For example, if you sell computers, there's *Computer Weekly*, *Computing*, etc. These are known as 'vertical industry' publications. However, there may also be many publications read by people who use the products of your industry – for computers this might include accountants, engineers, production managers. These are your 'horizontal' publications. List every vertical publication and horizontal industry publication, all the industry correspondents of national newspapers, all the freelance writers, anybody who might have an interest in your products or services, and fire off copies of all your releases to the lot of them. This could give you well over a hundred addresses.

Which method to choose

Although the sniper is more economical in terms of stationery, postage and time, we have tended to favour the shotgun method for our clients. Over the years we have often been pleasantly surprised at the results. For example, if you were a small company making machinery to produce sandwiches, would you fancy the chances of one of your stories appearing in the *Financial Times*? The *FT*'s industrial correspondent was on our client's press list, and one day it happened – and brought in a lot of very valuable, good quality enquiries. The same release was also sent to (and used by) the *Business Today* radio programme, where it was heard by a certain national store chain's sandwich buyer – who promptly instructed his suppliers to install our client's new piece of equipment on 26 production lines!

Where can you get press lists from? You can subscribe to services such as PIMS, PRADS and *The Editor*, who provide names, addresses and editors' and correspondents' names for just about every single publication in the UK. Some public libraries may have copies of them.

PRESS RELEASE STATIONERY

You'll need specially printed stationery on which to print your releases. The design is important, because it's the stationery that makes the first impression on an editor as he picks up a release off the pile on his desk. A couple of pointers:

◆ Don't use your letterhead stationery, the stuff you use for correspondence. Impress editors that you are taking press relations seriously, and produce something special for the job. It should be in line with your general corporate image and quite simple, with maybe your name and logo top left and wording such as

'Press Release', 'News Release' or 'Media Information' to the right, and your address in small type across the bottom of the page. Variations on this are OK, but do keep it simple and low-key.

♦ Use bog-standard A4 80gsm white copier paper, printed preferably in not more than two colours, and certainly no fancy gizmos like thermofaxing or embossing. To an editor, releases printed on heavy-weight tinted bond paper with four-colour embossed printing say 'small company trying to look big'. Press releases from one of the world's biggest companies go out on ordinary photocopier-type 80gsm white copy paper, with the IBM logo and 'News Release' printed in blue.

FEATURES MONITORING

Earlier on we mentioned 'feature articles'. Like the broadsheet newspapers, most trade and industrial maga-zines run one or more features in each issue. The publishers produce lists of these features well in advance, in the hope of attracting advertising. You will also be interested in them from an editorial point of view, as opportunities to 'sell' articles to the editor, so you need to establish a system that will get hold of features lists and action them in good time. Lists are usually available from publications' advertisement departments.

If you're using the shotgun system of distribution, don't waste time and effort trying to keep track of the features in *all* your magazines. Your distribution list for your press releases may be very long. We often deal with client distribution lists of more than 150, but for features monitoring we pick out a shortlist of (say) a dozen of the most-read magazines in the industry and focus on them. Which are the most-read? Media address lists such as PIMS will quote circulation figures; pick the top 12 or so.

Remember what we said earlier about deadlines? If a magazine is listing an interesting feature scheduled to appear in its November issue, the deadline for any copy you may want to submit could be early October. Start taking action a month before that, i.e. a good two months in advance of the issue. Decide what sort of article on the featured topic you or your in-house expert might be able to write. Then prepare a short synopsis of it, contact the editor, and ask him if an article along those lines would be interesting to him. If he says 'yes', ask (a) how many words he wants, and (b) what his copy deadline will be. If he says 'no', ask if there's anything else he might find useful – your 'corporate backgrounder', for example (see below).

CORPORATE BACKGROUNDER

This consists of an overview of your company and its products and services, and is specifically written for journalists who want to gain information about you quickly and easily. This could be for a feature they are putting together, in which they want to list examples of companies involved in the topic concerned.

It must *not* be a sales document listing your products in a froth of 'wonderfuls' and 'superbs', unless you want to irritate the hell out of the journalist or editor (they don't buy products, they buy *stories* – remember?). So the backgrounder is factual and informative, and written in a logical sort of order.

Start with a general overview of the company; for example, what it does, where it is based, how long it has been in business, how many people it employs (if the figure sounds impressive!), annual growth percentage (ditto) and so on. Then look at the market you are in – the sort of customer that buys your products, the size of the present demand, any statistics you may have about how fast the market is growing. Journalists love facts and figures about an industry. Finally detail your main products and services, pointing out any special or unique features about them without appearing to get over-excited about it.

Corporate backgrounders are also very useful for inclusion in press packs at exhibitions as well as in features work.

Getting Your Copy Published

Writing for the press is a discipline of its own and, before you put pen to paper, you need to know that there are styles of writing which are acceptable to editors and styles that are not. You may have to use a slightly different approach when writing for a trade or industry magazine than, say, for local newspapers but, by and large, different editors' stylistic likes and dislikes don't vary by that much.

So here are some tips from professionals who have been writing copy that editors have been finding acceptable for nearly a quarter of a century.

GIVE THEM *FACTS*

Journalists are hungry for facts and figures. If you are the industry expert you want them to believe you are, you will have facts and figures at your fingertips. **Quantify** wherever possible. Rather than writing vaguely about market surveys predicting a considerable increase in medium-term demand, much better to say (for example): 'A Dataquest survey carried out earlier this year indicated a 47 per cent growth in demand over the next two years'.

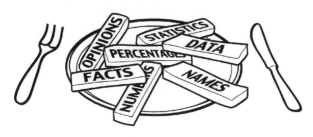

JOURNALISTS are HUNGRY FOR FACTS

Don't dress up your guesses as facts, and don't pick percentages out of the air. To you, saying '90 per cent of consumers' may be shorthand for 'almost all consumers'. To an editor, 90 per cent means just what it says: nine out of ten, and where did you get this figure from?

DON'T 'SELL' – THEY'RE NOT BUYING

The new-product press release that's written in the second person, as if the editor is a prospective customer ('You and your family will appreciate the SuperCleaner's smooth, silent operation...') is doomed. He doesn't buy products, he buys *stories*. And if he printed this story exactly as written, his magazine would appear to be directly endorsing the product, which he certainly will not do – that's the job of advertisements. Will he spare the time to go through it and amend it for you? Almost certainly not. The bin awaits.

MAKE IT SHORT AND SWEET

Forget what they taught you at evening classes about writing sophisticated and stylistic prose. Try for short, crisp sentences of no more than 25 words, written in good English, and paragraphs of no more than 10 lines. Focus on getting factual information over to the editor. Assume he has no sense of humour, so don't put in touches of satire or try to make it amusing.

ANTICIPATE QUESTIONS

Don't leave loose ends which raise questions. Example: You are launching a new product which works faster than its rivals. Your press release says that 'Harrison's new MaxiGizmo produces more widgets per hour than any other machine of its type'. This instantly raises the question, 'Wonderful, but *how many* per hour?' The editor thinks that his readers will want to know this. Wouldn't you, if you were reading it? And he may well wonder, why aren't you telling him? The only way to sort it out is to pick up the phone and ask you. Or, if he's busy, maybe he won't bother to use your story this time...

WEED OUT THE SUPERLATIVES

Industrial editors in particular detest superlatives. Sprinkling your editorial copy with adjectives like 'incredible', 'fantastic', 'exciting', 'wonderful', 'earth-shattering' will ensure that it hits the editorial bin almost without a second thought. 'Unique', 'new', 'user-friendly', 'flexible', 'cost-effective' and the like are generally OK, especially if backed by convincing facts and figures.

AVOID INITIAL CAPS

Editors generally do not use initial capital letters in job titles and names of departments. Thus, Sales Managers are sales managers, Marketing Departments are marketing departments. Even the sacred person of the Chairman will be demoted to chairman, and the Managing Director may be cut down to 'the md'. You don't want to give editors a job to do amending your copy, so adopt the same practice yourself. If any of your Very Important People check one of your draft releases and raise objections, show them a few magazine pages to prove your point.

OTHER STYLISTIC STUFF

Typefaces
Use a clean, easily readable typeface such as Arial or Times New Roman. Using fussy, decorative faces, joined-up scripts, etc. to make a press release look 'different' are generally not appreciated.

Brackets
Don't use them, except for the first time you mention a product or service acronym, e.g. 'Personal Identification Number (PIN)'. Use parenthetic commas instead, e.g., 'John Smith, 34, has joined the marketing team...' rather than 'John Smith (34) has joined...'.

Percentages
Write out in full, e.g. '20 per cent', not '20%'.

Numbers
Numbers up to nine are written out in full, e.g. 'We have added five new features...' After 10, use numerals.

Names of people
If you're a small and friendly outfit, it's tempting to use first names in releases announcing appointments, e.g. '... and Caroline will be responsible for....' In general, however, editors favour the more formal approach: '... and Caroline Jones will be...'. Solo surnames are

more acceptable than first names, e.g. '... and Smith will head up a team...'.

LAYOUT

Always **double-space** the lines on all editorial copy, to give the editor space to mark up amendments if necessary – certainly not less than 1.5 spaces. Single spacing between lines is one of those major irritants which says 'amateur PR', very loudly. Leave uncluttered one-inch left and right page margins for the same reason.

If the release runs to more than one page (try to keep it to no more than two pages), then at the bottom of the page you print '**/more**...' At the top of the second page, print an ellipsis '...' followed by the release heading, followed by '**cont 2/**'. For example: '...Harrisons appoints new sales director cont 2/'. The reason is that if the pages get separated, the editor can match them up again. And when he hands over your release to be typeset, the typesetter knows not to set words between slash marks.

At the end of the release copy, put '**-ends-**' or '**/ends/**' (no need to explain why!). After that, quote a contact name, phone number, fax number and email address in case the editor wants to query anything: 'For more information, please contact...'

And finally: **Never, ever, print on both sides of a page,** e.g. print page 2 of a press release on the back of page 1. It may help to save the rain forests, but unfortunately editors *never* turn pages over and look at the back...

$$\left(5 \right)$$

Telling Your News – Press Releases

We've said it before but it's worthwhile repeating here: **Press releases form the platform on which your entire press relations campaign will be based**. You start the campaign with them, and you try to send out at least one every month if possible.

Apart from briefing the press, there are several useful spin-offs you can get from press releases. For example, they come in handy as news items in your corporate newsletter or house magazine and you can quite easily convert some releases into 'Newsflash' leaflets for use in direct mail shots.

An increasing number of organisations are also putting copies of their releases on their website news pages – for an example of the benefits to be gained by doing this, see the press relations case study on 'Albert the Wonderloo' on page 104. Also, anyone scrolling down through the headings of all your releases, articles, etc. will be really impressed with how active and successful you are, even if they don't read them all!

Selecting good, newsworthy stories for press releasing is important, but the way you **present** them to the press is critical. When you are researching and writing news stories, you may find yourself trying to tell them as *you* would like them to appear in the press. Correct this suicidal tendency! The wording, the style, the 'shape' of the story, all must accord with what an **editor** would want to see, and which give him the least possible trouble if he is considering using it. Editors receive dozens of press releases every week, but they don't have enough space to use them all. Hence they have to make choices as to what they do with each one.

GETTING YOUR STORY ON THE PAGE

What are the choices open to an editor when he picks up your release? He has three basic options:

1. Use it in the issue he's currently putting together.

2. If there's no space for it at present, hold it pending for a future issue.

3. Bin it.

Remember, there's no appeal procedure! So when an editor's eye first alights on your press release, what is he looking for? How does he decide whether yours gets in, gets held over, or hits the bin? It takes only seconds for him to check the following.

Is there a story, and what is it?

Can he see at a glance what the story is? The editor needs to know what kind of story it is, so as to know where to put it in the magazine (see 'Writing for slots' below – and now you know the reason for putting headings on press releases!). If he has to battle his way through a literary jungle in an effort to discover the answer, well, a busy editor with lots of other material to choose from probably won't bother. On the other hand, if he can see that it's a good, worthwhile story, he may elbow someone else's out to put yours in.

Who *are* you?
Does the editor know you? Has he seen any stories from you before? If you're a complete newcomer, all other things being equal he may give his regular contributors priority if he's strapped for space. But if he likes what he sees, you might get held over to a later issue. And believe it, it does happen; we've seen a story appear in a magazine about nine months after we sent it to them. It was a personnel appointment story accompanied by a pic, and our client remarked that the release was so old yet he still looked so young!

Do I have to do any work on it?
If the editor understands what the story is but he has to rewrite your release, or contact you to resolve queries, this busy person may decide that the bin is the easiest solution. 'The best possible story for the least possible effort' is the ideal combination that your average editor is looking for. Give him both, and you've gained his respect – and probably a place in one of his forthcoming issues.

WHAT MAKES A STORY?
Most news items in trade and industry mags are of

general interest in a 'what's-happening-in-the-industry' kind of way, and are largely provided by way of press releases sent in by outfits just like yours. It certainly doesn't have to be an earth-shattering event which will have readers sitting on the edge of their seats – which is just as well for editors because there aren't many stories like this coming in to him regularly.

Here's a checklist of story categories for you to consider. A bit later on we'll look at how you would write each of them up.

Make your story fit a slot

Orders and installations
This could be a fairly large order you've just received, or an interesting one (first order for a new product you announced recently, your first ever export order, or a big-name customer like a multinational oil company or airline). This category would also embrace post-order 'installation' or 'delivery' stories.

A word of warning at this point: You must never write a story naming a third party (in this case, your customer) without getting the third party's approval to do so, and you certainly must *not* send the story out to the press without securing their unequivocal approval of the text. This is usually done either through the contact you have been talking to when you were researching the release, or through the customer's Press Office.

Some organisations (and particularly some government departments) are extremely fussy about confidentiality, and some have policies forbidding them from endorsing another company's products or services. If you come up against any of these, don't risk upsetting a customer by arguing with them. Better to bow out gracefully and find another story.

New products

This is a popular type of story with editors, especially if you can describe the product as what a journalist thinks of as 'new, free or amazing'. Also announce significant enhancements or redesigns to existing products – now more powerful, faster, reduced price, whatever.

Personnel appointments

Known in the trade as 'body shots', these are popular especially if they are customer-facing, e.g. area representative, sales/marketing manager, or senior folk such as CEOs and Board directors. Always try to send a captioned picture ('mug-shot') of the subject with body shots.

Exhibition attendance

If you will be showing at some well-known trade fair or exhibition, here's a story. A number of magazines run show features about a month beforehand, so send out a release about what you will be showing. Don't send out up-beat releases afterwards, saying how many people came on to your stand and how much interest was shown; it's not news. But if you grabbed a decent order or contract at the show – that's news!

General news

A loose category, this one, but not to be overlooked. For example, if you have appointed a new distributor in this country or overseas (or been appointed as one yourself), moved into new premises, seen your sales go up by a hefty percentage during a period when others are struggling, sponsored a well-known charitable event or sports team – that's news, too!

Beware, however, of putting out stories with a negative slant. 'A member of staff is leaving' (unless he/she is retiring after many years' service); 'we have withdrawn our sponsorship of X'; 'contrary to any rumours you may have heard, our financial position is sound'. Anything with a whiff of failure about it is open to be treated as bad news. A Cromwellian desire to paint yourself 'warts and all' may sound like a bold, open corporate policy; unfortunately, warts are bad news.

LATCH ON TO CURRENT RUNNING STORIES

You may gain quite a lot of mileage by latching on to a big story that's running in the press at the moment.

Here's an example. Some years ago one of our clients, a small and somewhat insignificant engineering company, managed to increase its turnover by about 30 per cent during a period when the national news pages were dominated by doom-and-gloom stories about the failing economy, depression, corporate failures, etc. We put out a simple news story announcing the 30 per cent increase. A small company doing better than the big boys in a recession was a happy story amidst the almost universally bad news, and the media started to beat a path to our client's door. Our only problem was how to fend off journalists who wanted to come and interview the client face to face, because we didn't want them to see just how small the company really was! The telephone can be a great blessing sometimes...

Similar things happened during the wars in the Falklands and the Gulf. The press contracted sustained bouts of war fever, and any alert PR person whose company had a product or service that was in any way connected with the Army, Navy or Air Force found an excuse to mention it in a press release. We know of one company that made a small computer device which was used in army tanks and, er, just happened to develop a fairly minor enhancement to it during the Falklands War. Good thinking, Batman, and the story deserved the good take-up it received.

So keep alert! Wars, floods, economic ups and downs, Olympic Games, general elections, flights to Mars, whatever's making headline news on the front pages – if you can find a way of latching on to it with a related story of your own, it may well be PR bonus time for you.

WRITE FOR SLOTS

Check the editorial pages of a selection of trade and industrial magazines and you'll see that different kinds of news items are usually grouped into sections, or 'slots'. For example, there will be one or more pages of general stories such as company mergers or takeovers, corporate results, distribution agreements, and so on – the news slot. There may also be a new products slot, an orders slot, an appointments slot, and so on. This slot principle is very important, because it places certain imperatives upon the press release writer.

> **The first imperative of the slot principle is: If your story doesn't obviously fit into a slot, it may not be used.**

Your release must start with a **heading** which immediately points the story towards one of the common slots in magazines. A release headed 'New sales director for Harrisons' is instantly identifiable as for the appointments slot, 'Harrisons win £2m order for...' is for the orders slot, etc. But what does the editor do with something headed 'Harrisons chairman slams government over-regulation'? It doesn't fit a slot, so out it goes.

> **The second imperative is: Never try to combine two stories in one press release.**

This is a common Beginner's Mistake, often justified on grounds of economy. However, it's false economy. For example: a release headed 'Harrisons moves into United States market, appoints new export sales manager'. A logical connection, perhaps, but this one release covers two slots: general news, and appointments. No editor wants the bother of re-shaping it into two separate stories, so it's possible that he won't use it at all. Besides, putting out two separate stories gives you the chance of two possible editorial appearances in each of your target magazines. So go on, splash out and hang the economics!

And the third imperative is: One story per organisation, per slot, per issue.

To avoid any appearance of favouritism, most editors take care not to pack slots in individual issues with several stories about one organisation. So if you send out three 'order' stories in quick succession, all in time for the next magazine issue, the editor will normally use only one of them. The choice of which one goes in (if any) will be at his discretion; it may not be the one you thought most important, and you've wasted the other two. The moral is: If you feel the urge to send out more than one story per week or month, **make sure they are aimed at different slots**.

'SHAPING' THE RELEASE
How you tell your stories – in terms of how the information is arranged into paragraphs – is very important indeed. Story 'shapes' will vary in detail with the type of story you are telling (see below), but the

fundamental order of things is almost always the same.

The heading says what the release is about (and what slot it's aimed at).

Paragraph One summarises the main essential point(s) of the story.

Paragraph Two expands it with more detail.

Paragraph Three continues the expansion, and includes any quotes.

Paragraphs Four, Five and so on can be used for more low-level routine information such as product specifications, delivery times etc.

The last paragraph (called the 'boilerplate') gives a brief summary of your organisation, what you do, etc.

Why shape is important
We have already discussed the criteria that an editor uses to choose one story rather than another. Assuming he chooses yours, he then applies one more yardstick to it: the available **space** in its slot, which may be restricted. If he has plenty of good stories, he may decide to use, say, 50 or so words from each one. He therefore has to prune, and he does this by reading downwards from Paragraph One and working through the following paragraphs until he's reached his desired wordage. Then he puts his pen through the rest of it.

Hence it is vital that the really important messages that you want to get across are contained in the first, and possibly the second, paragraphs.

Looking at some common magazine slots, press release shapes would look like this:

New product stories
Para. 1: What the product does that's new or unique, and for whom it does it.

Para. 2: How it does it – the clever technology.

Para. 3: How it fits into the market, its prospects – and maybe a positive quotation by your MD or marketing manager.

Para. 4: Specifications/sizes/colours available, delivery times, etc.

Para. 5: Boilerplate.

Appointment stories
Para. 1: Who has been appointed, job title, what he/she will do.

Para. 2: The appointee's previous relevant career (starting with the most recent job).

Para. 3: Quotation from MD linking appointment to corporate expansion plans, etc.

Para. 4: Boilerplate.

Order or installation stories
Para. 1: Who has ordered/installed what, the main benefits they will gain.

Para. 2: More information about the products/systems and how they will be used.

Para. 3: (If relevant) how the customer managed previously, plus a quote from the customer saying why they bought from you.

Para. 4: Boilerplate.

You'll find some examples of press releases written for different slots at the end of this chapter.

RESEARCHING PRESS RELEASES
It's very difficult, if not impossible, to write a meaningful press release without researching the facts beforehand. The time and effort required for research will vary – five minutes reading a simple product specification, half an hour on the phone to a talkative salesperson, eight phone calls to contact an elusive customer – but careful research always pays off. Here are some research guidelines.

Is there a story?
It sounds obvious, but do make sure that you know the basic facts before going to in-depth research. For instance, some excitable guy or gal in Marketing may tell you that Sproggs have just ordered a £1.2 million SuperGizmo

machine from your company – we must get a press release out immediately!

First, have a word with the front-line salesperson concerned. You may discover that the order hasn't actually been confirmed, so Sproggs won't want to talk to you just yet. Same with 'new product' stories; don't try to announce them while they're only a twinkle in the R&D manager's eye...

Get approval

Releases on subjects such as orders and distribution agreements involve other parties, and you *must* obtain their agreement in principle before researching and writing such stories. Ask nicely for this approval *before* starting your research, otherwise you won't get very far with it! You may have to approach the other party's Press Office or PR agency, and you will have to submit copy to the other party for final approval before the press release is distributed.

Incidentally, it can often help to get initial approval to write the release if you emphasise that you will be submitting the copy for approval before it goes out to the press – that nothing will appear in print before they approve it. It all may sound like a lot of fuss and bother between friends, but many a business friendship has been badly strained by one party taking the other for granted.

List your questions

We have said that you will almost invariably have to talk to someone to get the facts you need. There are few things more frustrating than finishing a telephone call to a customer to research an order story, for example, only to realise that you've forgotten to ask him for a comment on why he bought your equipment. So, before making contact, always draw up a really detailed questionnaire for that particular release, covering all the aspects of the story. This should even include details such as the correct spelling of the customer's name, and a prompt to ask for the customer's fax number or email address for sending him copy for approval (a reassuring touch with which to end the interview).

Just a tip from a couple of old hands in the game: On order/installation stories, don't take everything that your own salesperson tells you as gospel. When you talk to the customer, check what he's bought, and its value – sometimes you can actually get two different versions, which need to be back-checked with your organisation's sales records to establish which is correct.

A FINAL WORD OF WARNING

By this time you might be thinking that writing press releases to standard shapes sounds dead boring, and as neither you nor your products/services are boring, let's smash the mould and write really exciting releases which are so fizzy and different that editors will leap to their feet, cheering wildly, and use every wonderful word of them . . .

If such thoughts are taking shape in your mind, we beg of you – *forget the whole idea, right now.*

'Fizzy' releases have been tried countless times before, and almost invariably with disastrous results. The fact is that editors are, by and large, fairly unexcitable characters who really do like press releases written in these time-honoured formats, because it actually helps them to do their jobs more quickly and easily. So take our advice and don't try to reinvent the wheel – the old, boring round one is still working just fine.

SOME EXAMPLES OF PRESS RELEASES

1 Order or installation story

Leading widget maker installs Harrisons robotic spray finishing system
Boosts throughput by 70 per cent, improves finish consistency

Wigitech Limited, a major manufacturer of high quality coated widgets, has increased the throughput of its spray finishing process by some 70 per cent following the installation of a bespoke robotic system designed and supplied by Harrisons of Wolverhampton Ltd. The new system has also improved repeatability and consistency of finish quality.

The Harrisons solution employs a computer-controlled precision robotic spray system. The detailed parameters of all products to be spray finished are entered into the computer, and this achieves higher consistency of finish quality, batch after batch, compared with the previous manual spray system.

An increase in orders prompted Wigitech to automate their previous manual spray finishing process. Charles Jones, Wigitech production director, said: 'We asked several companies to quote, and we gave the contract to Harrisons because they were willing to get involved with our problem and get an understanding of what we were really trying to achieve. Others just wanted to sell us robots.'

The cost of the Harrisons solution, including spray booth, conveyor, robot, PC and software, was around £250,000.

All Harrisons robotic spray systems are developed using high speed, high precision robots, suitable for spray applications in hazardous Zone 1 & 2 environments. The unique benefits of these robotic systems include the company's programming software utility, mountability of robots in any articulation, repeatable and exacting modular spray segments, high precision motion and trajectory control, and total reliability.

[Wigitech boilerplate paragraph]

[Harrisons boilerplate paragraph]

-ends-

Release date: 20th March 2003
For pictures or more information, please contact:
George Gregory, Harrisons of Wolverhampton Ltd
Tel: 01234 567891 Fax: 01234 567892
E-mail: ggregory@harrisonsrobot.co.uk

2 Appointment release ('body shot')

> ### Jim Johnson joins Harrisons as senior sales support engineer
>
> Harrisons of Wolverhampton Ltd, a leading developer of industrial robotic systems, has appointed Jim Johnson, 42, as senior sales support engineer. He will support users of Harrisons' range of high-speed robotic welding and finishing systems in the motor manufacturing and general engineering industries, mainly in the North of England and Scotland.
>
> Johnson has been in the engineering industry all his working life. Before joining Harrisons he spent nine years with Painton Systems, first as a service engineer and, latterly, as senior sales engineering manager marketing Painton's spray and electrostatic coating devices. He has also worked for Screwfeed Ltd on engineering support for product assembly line systems.
>
> Robert Harrison, Harrisons managing director, said: 'We welcome Jim Johnson as a very valuable addition to our technical team. In particular, his experience of spray coating systems will be appreciated by the growing number of Harrisons system users.'
>
> [Harrisons boilerplate paragraph]
>
> -ends-
>
> Release date: 4th September 2001
> For pictures or more information, please contact:
> George Gregory, Harrisons of Wolverhampton Ltd
> Tel: 01234 567891 Fax: 01234 567892
> E-mail: ggregory@harrisonsrobot.co.uk

3 New product or new service release

**Harrisons announces new robotic spray system
with unique logistics control
Also includes built-in nozzle checking system**

Harrisons of Wolverhampton Ltd, a leading developer of industrial robotic systems, has launched Intellispray, a new robotic spray finishing system with a uniquely high level of system intelligence for component manufacturers and finishers. Intellispray automatically adjusts nozzle settings and spray volumes to suit the individual products being sprayed, and their throughput speeds, and this can be applied to any one of up to 250 different products stored within the system's product memory.

Nozzles on all spray finish systems become clogged under certain circumstances and, to ensure consistent high quality on long spray runs, Intellispray provides for programming of nozzle checks at predetermined intervals. The time for a nozzle check is signalled by a blue flashing light; failure to conduct the check within a prescribed time limit will set off an audible alarm and a red alarm lamp.

Harvey Williams, development director at Harrisons of Wolverhampton, commented: 'Now, for the first time, component manufacturers can benefit from a fully automated self-adjusting finishing system. Shopfloor trials of Intellispray have indicated possible throughput increases of up to 60 per cent over a range of different products.'

All Harrisons robotic spray systems are developed using high speed, high precision robots, suitable for spray applications in hazardous Zone 1 & 2 environments. The unique benefits of these robotic systems include the company's programming software utility, mountability of robots in any articulation, repeatable and exacting modular spray segments, high precision motion and trajectory control, and total reliability.

Standard range Harrisons spray finish systems can all be customised to suit individual customers' needs, and Harrisons can also develop systems to meet specialised industrial requirements.

[Harrisons boilerplate paragraph]

-ends-

Release date: 9th January 2004
For pictures or more information, please contact:
George Gregory, Harrisons of Wolverhampton Ltd
Tel: 01234 567891 Fax: 01234 567892
E-mail: ggregory@harrisonsrobot.co.uk

4 Exhibition release

**Harrisons to show new Intellispray robotic finishing system for first time at Production and Processing exhibition
National Exhibition Centre, 15th–20th May 2004
Stand 155**

On Stand 155 at this year's Production and Processing exhibition, Harrisons of Wolverhampton Ltd will give the first public demonstrations of its recently-announced Intellispray, a new robotic spray finishing system with a uniquely high level of system intelligence for component manufacturers and finishers. Intellispray automatically adjusts nozzle settings and spray volumes to suit the individual products being sprayed, and their throughput speeds, and this can be applied to any one of up to 250 different products stored within the system's product memory.

Nozzles on all spray finish systems become clogged under certain circumstances and, to ensure consistent high quality on long spray runs, Intellispray provides for programming of nozzle checks at predetermined intervals. The time for a nozzle check is signalled by a blue flashing light; failure to conduct the check within a prescribed time limit will set off an audible alarm and a red alarm lamp.

Harrisons' stand will also feature examples from its standard range of robotic spray finishing and welding systems, and engineers will be available to discuss individual finishing and welding problems with visitors to the stand.

All Harrisons robotic spray systems are developed using high speed, high precision robots, suitable for spray applications in hazardous Zone 1 & 2 environments. The unique benefits of these robotic systems include the company's programming software utility, mountability of robots in any articulation, repeatable and exacting modular spray segments, high precision motion and trajectory control, and total reliability.

Standard range Harrisons spray finish systems can all be customised to suit individual customers' needs, and Harrisons can also develop systems to meet specialised industrial requirements.

[Harrisons boilerplate paragraph]

-ends-

Release date: 6th March 2004
For pictures or more information, please contact:
George Gregory, Harrisons of Wolverhampton Ltd
Tel: 01234 567891 Fax: 01234 567892
E-mail: ggregory@harrisonsrobot.co.uk

5 General news release

Harrisons buck manufacturing industry's gloom and doom
Announces largest ever order book – up 85 per cent on 2003

At a time when the UK manufacturing industry generally is reporting low levels of business, Harrisons of Wolverhampton Ltd is currently enjoying the largest order book in the company's history. The value of orders in hand at the end of January 2004 topped £960,000 – 85 per cent up on £520,000 at the same time last year – and the company is looking for more staff to support the rapid increase in its business.

Harrisons of Wolverhampton specialises in spray finish and welding solutions using robotics, data capture techniques, pneumatics and other advanced technologies. The company designs and builds machines for a very wide range of industries, and claims that the increase in business has come from all sectors. As a result, Harrisons is now actively looking for project engineers, designers and software engineers to join its existing team.

'A general lack of confidence among manufacturers tends to result in reduced investment in production equipment,' says Harrisons managing director, Robert Harrison. 'Those who are still investing demand the most cost-effective solutions, solutions that really work for them. Many of our recent orders didn't result from price cutting – our customers felt that we had the resources to solve their problems effectively, bring in projects successfully, and provide expert technical back-up.'

All Harrisons robotic spray systems are developed using high speed, high precision robots, suitable for spray applications in hazardous Zone 1 & 2 environments. The unique benefits of these robotic systems include the company's programming software utility, mountability of robots in any articulation, repeatable and exacting modular spray segments, high precision motion and trajectory control, and total reliability.

Standard range Harrisons spray finish systems can all be customised to suit individual customers' needs, and Harrisons can also develop systems to meet specialised industrial requirements.

[Harrisons boilerplate paragraph]

-ends-

Release date: 24th February 2004
For pictures or more information, please contact:
George Gregory, Harrisons of Wolverhampton Ltd
Tel: 01234 567891 Fax: 01234 567892
E-mail: ggregory@harrisonsrobot.co.uk

Becoming an Industry Guru – Articles

When you've sent out a variety of press releases, so that editors have been able to build up an image of a sound company that knows its technology and its marketplace, it will be time to think about trying to place **articles** with some of your key target publications. What you are looking for are opportunities to put one of your people in front of your marketplace as an expert in his field – an industry guru – with all the prestige that this can gain for your company in the eyes of your customers.

First, let's be clear what we mean by the word 'article'.

A surprisingly large number of people, when they first become involved with press relations, refer to press releases as articles. *You mustn't be one of them*, particularly when talking to a journalist, because there's a world of difference between the two.

As we have seen in previous pages, a press release is a relatively short piece (200–250 words, perhaps) announcing a single item of news; it will be sent out to a whole raft of publications. On the other hand, an article may vary in length between about 750 and 2,000 words; it will be exclusive to one publication, and will probably take an in-depth look at, say, a particular technology or the way a market is developing. If it looks at a specific problem and the way it was solved it's called a case study, or case history, and we'll deal with them in the next chapter.

To get an article published there are three steps you must take. These are:

1. Find a specific opportunity for an article.

2. Persuade an editor to take it.

3. Write it in a way that the editor will find acceptable.

FINDING ARTICLE OPPORTUNITIES

Features lists

The best way to find an opportunity for an article is by monitoring your key magazines' features lists. You may remember reading about features monitoring in Chapter 3, and perhaps you are monitoring them already. However, if it didn't fully register at the time, please mark this page, nip back to page 21, read it afresh, and return.

Welcome back!

Your magazines' features lists should provide a whole cornucopia of goodies to choose from. Throughout the year a food industry magazine, for example, will plan features on almost any subject you can think of –

ingredients, hygiene, meat processing, dairy products, packaging materials, conveyors, bag filling, labelling, computerised management systems, quality control pro- cedures, refrigerated distribution, protective clothing, etc. Somewhere in your trade magazines' annual features lists there are bound to be subjects on which your company can provide well-informed expert opinion.

Go with a running topic

As well as studying features lists, try to read your key magazines regularly. Apart from their planned feature subjects, one or more of them may have rabbited on over two or more issues about a particular subject which their editors obviously find interesting. Could one of your people make a useful contribution to the debate?

Meet the deadline

Do please note what we said earlier about the need to **meet deadlines**. Take action in good time, remembering to allow plenty of time for the actual writing of the article. However well-informed they may be, very few busy people who are not professional writers would be able to produce 1,500 words of informative and polished copy in less than about three or four days. So if the absolute deadline is the day after tomorrow, it's probably best to forget that one and go for something later in the year.

By the way, here's a useful tip on deadlines. If the features list shows a copy deadline date that is very close – or if you are struggling to meet an already agreed deadline – an editor *may* be prepared to stretch it by a few days. Many editors have a natural inclination to give themselves a little more leeway than strictly necessary. Even so, please don't ask for more time unless you really need it, and always ask as early as possible. Better to earn a reputation for reliability than for regular cliff-hanging!

Say something interesting

You've been through the features lists and a subject has caught your eye for an issue about two or three months away. What now? Don't rush to phone the editor just yet. First, make sure you (or one of your company's experts) will be able to come up with **a topic relevant to that feature**, and write an article which will say something **new and interesting** about it, and **sustain that interest** for maybe 1,500 words.

So, you have a topic for an article, you have someone who can write about it intelligently and interestingly, and you should have reasonable time in which to write it. On to the next stage:

PLACING ARTICLES

Phone your target editor. In a businesslike way, explain who you are and what your company does – hopefully you might be able to slip him a pleasant 'thank you' for using your last press release. Then refer to the name and date of his feature, and ask if he'd be interested in an article looking at Aspects x, y and z of that subject, because your company has someone with good in-depth knowledge of them.

This can prompt one of several initial reactions. One, of course, is 'Sorry, but...' (we already have enough contributors, or we have someone writing about that already, or we aren't going to cover Aspects x, y and z in this feature, or whatever). Disappointing, but it's nothing personal, so try again another time.

However, let's assume that the editor shows some degree of interest. If so, you will be facing one of two basic situations. Either the editor knows what he wants, or he's open to suggestions. You won't be left in doubt for very long about which situation you are dealing with.

Give the editor what he wants

The knowing editor may briskly tell you that he'd be interested in an article covering Aspects a, b and c, but *not* x, y and z. Be honest! If you know you can't come up to scratch on Aspects a, b and c, admit it and retire gracefully. Whatever you do, *don't* say yes to abc and then submit an article based on xyz in the hope that the editor will relent and accept it. He will be very annoyed indeed and, if you've also submitted it too late for him to commission another piece to fill the space in his magazine, he will possibly refuse to have anything more to do with you, ever.

Synopses

An editor who hasn't finalised a plan for the feature, and is open to suggestions, may say that Aspect x sounds quite interesting and could you submit a synopsis of what you propose to write.

Here, your answer *must* be yes. If he's never seen an article (as opposed to a press release) from you before, how does he know what sort of writer you are? A nice crisp synopsis of about 50–100 words, setting out the case your article will make, the main points you will cover, and possibly the qualifications of the author, will go a long way towards creating confidence in the editorial mind.

The other value of a synopsis is that, once it has been accepted by the editor, it acts as a large chunk of the vital **brief** for the article.

Keep to the brief

Whatever type of editor you are dealing with, the negotiation should if possible result in a clear brief for the article that is understood and agreed by all parties, and to which the writer must adhere. Last-minute arguments about whether or not the article you've submitted has been written to the brief can get quite acrimonious; do try to avoid them.

The brief for the article should include:

◆ a list of the basic topics to be covered (and possibly those not to be covered)

◆ whether the article may be by-lined with the author's name

◆ whether the article must be 'generic', i.e. not pushing your company and its products and services

◆ the number of words required

◆ whether pictures are wanted, and how many

◆ the deadline date for submission of copy.

One last thing on article briefings. Unless you have one already, **ask the editor to send you a copy of the magazine** so that you can get a feel for its layout and style. Do they use shortish or longish titles? Witty titles? By-lines? Introductions? Cross-heads in the main body of the article? Are the articles generally rather academic or 'not exactly rocket science'? The editor will normally be very happy to send you a copy and, because such a request is one of the marks of a professional writer, you may boost his confidence in you and thus score a nice little Brownie point with him for the future.

So we have a topic we know lots about, an editor willing to take an article about it, a briefing, a deadline date and a copy of the magazine we're writing for. Now sharpen your pencil, because it's time for the creative bit . . .

WRITING THE ARTICLE

Article shape
Like press releases, articles are usually written in a certain format – they have a **shape**. Typically the shape of an article might be:

Title. Attracts reader attention and indicates the subject.

By-line. Author's name, plus title, qualifications and organisation where appropriate.

Introduction. Two or three lines before the main article begins, setting out the general theme (but note: not all publications use introductions).

First paragraph. This introduces the main points to be discussed and/or the main tenor of the argument. It may also hint at the conclusion.

Second paragraph. A good place for useful background information, e.g. how a situation or market has developed over a period of time and where it stands now, results of independent surveys, forecasts of future development. This is the paragraph you can use to feed editors' love of facts and figures, and hopefully it will also provoke reader comments such as 'by heck, this chap knows his stuff!'

Further paragraphs. Move on from the facts to develop the subject/argument in a logical, factual and easy-to-follow way, working up to the:

Conclusion. Summarises the author's views and/or recommendations.

Article planning

Once you've got a number of successful articles under your belt, you may find that you can stick to a brief, develop an argument logically, keep within wordage limits, etc., almost without thinking about it. However, in the beginning – and for some people, for the whole of their writing careers! – it's highly advisable to map out a **plan** for the article first. When you've done it, check it carefully to make sure it fits the brief. Then try to stick to the plan as far as possible while you are writing the article itself.

Get some scrap paper and jot down the points that you will want to cover in the article. Think carefully about the arguments you intend to make and the factors you intend to include. As the various points occur to you, list them. Also list any facts and figures or references to sources of information that you might use; these could include quotations from speeches or recent newspaper or TV reports, government statistics, professional market surveys, books, and so on.

Now you've assembled the kit of parts, you can start putting the plan together.

At this point, you may experience an overwhelming temptation to begin by composing a clever, memorable title for your masterpiece. Resist this. A title is not necessary at this point. It can take ages to devise one that you're happy with, and you really need to focus on the priorities, i.e. the shape and contents. If a title hasn't already occurred to you beforehand, leave it until you've finished the article; by that time, one may have come to mind. The same goes for the introduction, if you are going to have one.

Begin by dividing up the proposed article into broad sections. A good way of doing this is by establishing section headings, called 'cross-heads', and listing under them the relevant points you intend to make in those areas. It's also a good discipline to include, in your notes for each section, an approximate wordage allowance.

Article planning – example

We were commissioned to write an article on behalf of a firm of hydrological engineers on the subject of flooding and flood control, especially in urban areas. The case we had to make was for a greater involvement of hydrological engineers (of course!) in the urban planning process, and improved flood control and drainage systems. The magazine's readership consisted mainly of professional engineers and surveyors.

The first section talked about rivers being natural waste water disposal channels, the increasing strains imposed on them from urban developments, a quotation from a DEFRA report about the number of properties located in flood plains, and a bit about the damage caused by flooding.

The second section was given a cross-head: 'Urbanisation encourages flooding'. Under this we developed the theme of how urbanisation creates flood control problems, listing reasons such as rainwater being less able to soak away into the ground in a town as it does in the countryside, reduction of natural areas available for water storage, and so on.

The next sections, now that we had detailed the problems, needed to point to possible ways to minimise the problems of flooding in urban areas, relevant regulations, and the latest developments in this area. The main lines of approach were (1) Development Siting and Planning, (2) Sustainable Drainage Systems, and (3) River Engineering and Management, so we used these three approaches as our next three cross-heads, listing various ways forward under each of them.

Having stated the facts and made our case, the last paragraph drew **the conclusion** that flooding is not a simple problem with one simple answer, but that the effects of flooding can be minimised if developers, planners, engineers, etc. combine to take a holistic approach to it.

The article was to be **by-lined** to our client company's managing director (the by-line also to include his academic and institutional qualifications) and his pic. No **introduction** was needed; we looked at the magazine and found that it didn't use them.

And in case you're on the edge of your seat wondering what we finally chose as a **title**, it was: '**When the rains drain mainly to the plain**'. Editors don't always use the title you have so lovingly created (editors also get creative instincts sometimes), but he used that one!

SOME USEFUL TIPS

Writing style

All writers develop their own particular style. *Vive la différence!* If all authors expressed themselves in exactly the same way, reading would be a pretty boring occupation. What you need to develop is a style which will be found acceptable by the editors of magazines in your field. It's very much a matter of 'horses for courses'. An article written in the style of the late Barbara Cartland might be welcomed by *Woman's World*, but the same style used for an article in *Engineering Today* would go down like the proverbial concrete fish.

Try to develop a style that is attractive and easy to read (concentration spans are short these days), and informative (to maintain your readers' interest). How? You can learn a lot from others in the writing business. Start reading the articles in your target press critically, as if you had to award them marks out of ten – not for their content but for their **readability factor**. Ask yourself, did I enjoy reading it? If so, why? Did I dislike anything about it, and if so, what? We've all read newspaper and magazine articles which, for one reason or another, we've found to be a turn-off. Learn from them; don't make the same mistakes.

Here are a few basic style pointers which might help.

Avoid **Waffle Syndrome**. If you are falling noticeably short of the wordage target, it's much better to finish at a hundred or two less and offer the editor a couple of good pics to fill the gap rather than trying to pad it out with lots of unnecessary words. The satirical magazine *Private Eye* sometimes features items by an imaginary journalist called 'Phil Space', who writes totally irrelevant waffly copy just to fill up the space his editor has allotted him. Don't spoil a good piece with waffle just to make the wordage target – an all-too-common practice, even among some journalists.

Another potential pitfall is the **Ego Trip Trap**. Even the most experienced commercial writer can sometimes lose sight of the needs of his readership in a pink-tinted haze of wonder at the cleverness, wit and sophistication of his immortal prose. The Ego Trip Trap victim is under the delusion that his readers don't want boring old facts and figures; they just want his wonderful words. The first person singular features large on the pages. The results of falling into an ETT are usually similar to those of the Waffle Syndrome; an article that turns the reader off after the first few paragraphs.

SHORT SENTENCES are BEST

As with press releases, try to use fairly short, **easy-to-read words** assembled into **crisp sentences** of not more than about 20 words. Don't be afraid to make **paragraph breaks frequently;** certainly, bringing in a new factor or changing the course of your argument calls for a new paragraph. **Cross-heads** (paragraph headings) can also be very useful to lead the reader on from one section or line of thought to another but, of course, only if the magazine you are writing for uses them.

The ultimate test of writing style is an editor's 'yes' or 'no'. But before putting an article to that test, be your own sternest critic. Read through what you have written and then ask yourself, with total honesty – *would anyone really want to read this stuff?* Then ask a friend or colleague to read it and give you an honest opinion. Don't argue with them, and be truly prepared to make changes if necessary.

Many writers find it very difficult to accept that their words of wisdom do not come down from Mount Sinai, indelibly inscribed on tablets of stone. Reaching that acceptance is a humbling, but very important, step forward in a writer's career.

'Generic' articles

Sometimes an editor will ask you to write what's called a generic article, which means that you are not supposed to give pride of place to your own products or services. You will probably be allowed to by-line the piece with name, title and company of the author, but product or corporate puffs in the body copy are not acceptable. This frustrating limitation is often imposed by, for example, house journals of professional associations (or, dare we say it, publications with a lively sense of their own importance in their field!).

One way round the generic straightjacket that we have discovered over the years is to use you or your products as *examples* to illustrate what you are talking about. With luck and a following wind, the editor will overlook the fact that you haven't mentioned anyone else as examples. In our hydraulic engineering flood control article, for instance, we might have talked about the need for computer-based modelling systems in river management, and dropped in something like 'engineering consultants such as Watertech have developed software systems that will...' and so on.

It's probably best to use these 'examples' later rather than earlier in the piece – it may help to lull the editor into a false sense of security...

Wordage limits

The wordage figure that the editor gives you as part of your briefing is based on the space he has available for your article. Hence, when a magazine editor tells you he wants 'about 1,500 words with a couple of pics please' he has probably handed you about two pages of his magazine to fill – no more, no less. Send him 2,000 words and he's got to cut the article down to size; 1,000 give him a big hole to fill. Either way, he will not be a happy bunny – you've let him down, given him a problem which he shouldn't have to deal with. If you have noticeably over- or under-run, it's up to you to adjust this before you submit the article. And do give the editor the final word count when you send it in.

Having said this, most editors would turn a blind eye to, say, four or five per cent over or under wordage. Hence, if the target is 1,500 and you've written about 1,550 or 1,430, you could probably submit it with a clear conscience.

Check the word count regularly against your plan as the article progresses; it's not a good idea to leave it until the conclusion to discover that you have to cut or add several hundred words! In the old days making regular word counts was a bit of a pain, but the 'word count' gizmo in today's word-processing software makes it a five-second job.

'If it Worked for Them . . .'
– Case Studies

Case studies are popular with many editors because readers like them. And why do readers like them? Because a case study:

- examines a specific problem experienced by an organisation

- describes how it was solved

- sets out the benefits that the solution provided.

If the problem is a fairly common one – say, production lagging behind orders, administrative muddles, or a need for better customer communication – quite a few readers may identify with it, and be interested to know how it was solved. 'We've got a problem like that, and if the solution worked for them . . .'

Hence, case studies should be popular with you too, because they are great opportunities for you to promote your organisation and its products and services with a positive success story. Unlike articles, an editor really cannot insist on a case study being anonymous or 'generic' because readers will want to know who implemented the solution, how, and with what equipment or know-how. So, if you don't take too many liberties, you can splash yourself about a bit.

Much of what we said in the previous chapter about articles applies equally to case studies – finding opportunities for them, placing them, making a plan, writing them, and the general pointers on style, keeping to wordage, etc. – so we won't bore you by repeating it. However, there are some notable differences in approach and shape.

POINTS TO CONSIDER
Here are a few extra points to consider when approaching case studies:

Research by visit
Researching an article is normally a desk-bound occupation, whereas researching a case study is best done by way of a personal visit to the site if at all practical. This can involve quite a lot of non-productive travelling time, but a visit allows you to get a 'feel' for the customer and his company, to talk to the people involved and get some good upbeat quotes, and to check possible subjects for photography (or to take pics yourself, if you're competent in that department).

Be patient
Like wines, curries and authors, case studies often improve with a little ageing. Patience is a virtue here. Better not to write a case study immediately after a

problem solution goes live; wait until the benefits have had time to come through and be fully appreciated. Three months? Six, perhaps?

Get ideas from releases
'Order' or 'installation' press release stories can often prompt ideas for future case studies. Many's the time we have written up an order story for a client, thought 'That would make a good case study', and made a note to talk to the customer again in a few months' time. However, before that talk, always check:

Make sure the customer's happy
Writing a case study depends entirely on the goodwill of the customer concerned. You will have to get (1) his permission to do it, (2) his cooperation during the research process, and (3) his approval of the final copy before publication. He may have been deliriously happy with the solution just after it was implemented; now, four months down the line, there could be a technical glitch or a service problem that your outfit hasn't managed to put right yet. Do talk to your sales and support people before approaching a customer, because asking him effectively to endorse your company might be rubbing salt into an open wound at that point!

CASE STUDY SHAPE
The shape of a case study is different from that of an article. In an article, you are typically taking a **topic** and developing a discussion in terms of background, present situation and possible future developments. On the other hand, a case study examines a practical **problem** experi-

enced by a named organisation, describes the solution and how it was arrived at, and details the benefits provided by the solution.

The shape of a typical case study will, therefore, look something like this:

Title. This attracts reader attention and indicates the theme of the case study.

By-line. It could be as for an article, but this is unlikely; by-lines are not often used in case studies. This is not necessarily a Bad Thing, because without a by-line the study can look as if it was written by an independent journalist employed by the publication. However, an author's name may be mentioned in the:

Introduction. Two or three lines expanding the title theme. It might include a reference to the author, such as 'Charles Brown looks at an organisation that...' or similar.

First section. Sets the scene. Describe the organisation being studied – what it does, how big it is, anything particularly interesting about it, etc.

Second section. Introduces the problem it had. Go from the general to the particular. First, outline the nature of the problem; then give details of what was happening, and the negative impact it was having.

Third section. The build-up to the crunch point – the moment when it was decided that the problem had to be solved. Any particular event(s) which prompted that decision.

Fourth section. How the organisation went about tackling the problem to arrive at a solution. What the solution was.

Fifth section. Detail the solution and how it was implemented.

Last paragraph or two. Detail the benefits the organisation has gained from the solution. Include positive quotations from members of the organisation's staff wherever possible.

Conclusion. Could be an upbeat (but believable!) quote by the customer summing up the overall benefits: 'Yes, the change to x was an upheaval, but the extra business we've gained has more than justified...' or something on those lines. However, if you can't come up with a neat, crisp conclusion, best leave it out.

CASE STUDY SHAPE – EXAMPLE

On behalf of an international manufacturer of telecoms equipment we were asked to write a case study based on problems that had been experienced by a ferry operator with handling increasing volumes of incoming enquiries and bookings from prospective passengers. Let's call the ferry operator 'the Line'. In this instance the case study hadn't yet been placed with a magazine; we were writing it 'on spec', so we set ourselves a wordage limit of 1,500. It went like this:

Title. An anodyne one for a so-far unknown magazine – 'Call Centre Smooths Ferry Crossings'.

Introduction. Three lines introducing the subject of the case study and whetting appetites by mentioning that more than 2 million enquiries and bookings a year were now being handled profitably.

First paragraph. Basic facts about the Line, how successful it had been, and how its business was expanding.

Second section. The existing telephone call centre. Problems posed by handling increasing volumes of calls, and the need to adopt a more marketing-oriented approach to enquiries and bookings.

Third section. Crunch time. The Line started another cross-Channel route, calls up to 1.8m a year, more product offerings to sell, call centre not coping. Quote by call centre manager describing pressure from departments.

Fourth section. How the Line went about looking for a new call centre. The criteria and specifications they set out. Tendering. Order placed with our client for latest state-of-the-art call centre. Quote from call centre manager explaining why our client won the contract.

Fifth section. Details of the call centre. Easier to use. Flexible working. Supports more agents. 24-hour support by our client.

Last paragraph. The benefits. Improved call handling. Better workload scheduling. Ability to accept a planned new reservations system and interaction with the Line's websites. Quote from call centre manager about staff numbers, training programmes, etc.

Conclusion. Calls now up to 2m a year. Quote from call centre manager about our client being innovative, close support, relationship good.

We finally wrote 1,490 words. Our client's name was mentioned eight times, and the proprietary names of its equipment scored 13.

PREPARING FOR THE CASE STUDY

Before packing your sandwiches and setting out on your expedition to Torquay or Aberdeen or wherever, you will need to prepare both yourself and the subject organisation. Remember: the people you are going to see are not obliged to help you; they are doing you a favour. You can repay them by being well-prepared, efficient and unobtrusive, and taking up as little of their time as possible. For example, look up their website if they have one – it's often a good source of basic information on the company and its products and services, and can save several minutes of face-to-face question time.

Having targeted the subject of your proposed case study, go through this basic checklist of things to do before appearing on their doorstep.

preparation
is never wasted

Decide what the story is
Ask the sales person dealing with that customer for a brief run-down on the history – the company, where it is, what it does, the problem, how it was solved, any 'high spots' in the solution that are worthy of exploration.

Find out who you should talk to
Ask the sales person for at least one contact name and phone number, preferably someone senior who can give permission for the case study to be done. It's also useful to have the name of someone who is involved in the day-to-day running of the department or section where the solution was installed.

Phone the most senior customer contact

Explain who you are and what you would like to do. Reassure him that he will have final approval of the case study before publication – 'nothing will go out without your say-so'. If he is willing, tell him how much of his time you would need (as a guide, most of the case studies we have written have taken between one and one-and-a-half hours face-to-face research) and agree a time and date for you to visit him. He may suggest that you interview someone in the relevant department instead; go along with it, but say that you'd also like to have the opportunity to meet him during your visit if he's available (nice to get an off-the-cuff quote from Mr Big while you're there).

If you are unsure of their location, check their website to see if there's a map or directions. If not, ask them to send you directions by post, fax or email, including a map if possible. Quite a lot of organisations have these already printed up and ready, so it's no problem for them.

Prepare your questions

As if you were researching a press release, prepare a detailed questionnaire before your visit. It keeps the interview on track and helps it to go smoothly, and it can avoid embarrassment later. Your friends won't be too happy if, after they've given you an hour or two of their valuable time, you phone several times in the next few days with 'I'm afraid I forgot to ask you' type questions. Don't forget to include 'pics' as one of your prompts.

List your questions using the sections outlined above as a prompt, and with luck you'll cover everything in one hit.

ON THE DAY
Your hosts are doing you a favour, so do what you can to fit in with them and minimise any problems your presence might cause. Here are some helpful hints for the day:

Check that you've got everything
Before you go: Questionnaire? Notebook or clipboard with plenty of paper? At least two pens? Your business cards? The directions and the map? Your mobile? Your host's telephone number?

Look smart
Maybe you are going there as a writer, but a business executive or civil servant really won't appreciate the Bohemian sweat shirt, jeans and sandals one little bit. Dress smartly as you would for the office.

Try to arrive on time
They will have allocated a time-slot for you. So, if your train's running late or you are stuck in a jam on the M6, use your mobile to give them reasonable warning that sorry, you may be delayed, and hopefully this won't be a problem for them.

Be a document collector
If you have to sit in a waiting room for a while on arrival, there will sometimes be a display of documentation such as corporate and product brochures, copies of company newsletters or magazines. Pop a few into your briefcase because they may fill an information gap, or provide

something eye-catching about the company when you come to write your piece, or reveal the existence of a good pic you could use to illustrate the case study.

Concentrate on the job

Some case study interviewers start by trying to make polite conversation, hoping that it will put the victim (or themselves!) at their ease: 'What a pleasant view you have from this window, Mrs Jones' type of thing. It may actually have the opposite effect. Mrs Jones is being charming as always, but is secretly keen to get this done and move on to something more productive. So, when the usual did-you-have-a-good-journey and would-you-like-tea-or-coffee exchanges are over, take out your pen and questionnaire briskly, and get stuck in.

Fish for quotable quotes

Case studies always benefit from positive user quotations, so fish for some. When the interviewee is describing how the solution was implemented, for example, casually ask 'Did our people and yours work well together?' When she is talking about a particular benefit they've gained: 'That sounds like a better result than you expected, Mrs Jones.'

Dig for facts and figures

In case studies, readers like to have detailed figures wherever possible. If your interviewee tells you that 'it was taking staff a long time to answer incoming phone calls', ask: 'About how long, do you know?' 'Production increased dramatically': ask, 'What sort of percentage?'

Case studies can be quite fun to do; believe us, we've written dozens of them! You get to visit those faraway places with strange-sounding names, you meet some interesting people, and the factual 'reporting' style of the case study can make writing it easier and less taxing than an article calling for opinions and new thinking (articles, by the way, are sometimes called 'think pieces').

8

Face to Face – Working with Journalists

Earlier on, we said that most of your contact with editors and journalists will be by way of the *written* word – that you won't very often find yourself actually face to face with the ladies and gentlemen of the press. However, there are times when you will find yourself faced with the prospect of talking directly to a journalist, either in person or by telephone. This may range from a brief phone call from an editor to raise a simple query about something in your latest press release ('I've got everything I need except the price – how much are they?'), through a more extended interview perhaps to get your views on a story that's going the rounds, to a full-blown press conference.

Before we look at the various possibilities in detail, there are a few things you need to have very firmly in mind before getting involved with face-to-face contacts with the press. Unlike a written statement such as a press release, which you can ponder over and amend at leisure before you issue it, the spoken words you nervously blurt out to a journalist will be very difficult to redeem or withdraw. Hence it's very much a case of engaging the brain before putting the mouth in gear, and knowing the basic rules of the direct encounter – whatever the situation. Having said this, comfort yourself with the thought that an alert PR person can often use the face-to-face situation to good effect.

POINTS TO REMEMBER
So let's start with some Words of Wisdom for dealing directly with the press.

Establish a corporate policy for handling the media
This is important. You need to nominate one or two first-line contact people who will initially handle **all** incoming enquiries from the press, and make sure that everyone knows who they are. It must also be made very clear to all staff (ideally in their contracts of employment) that only certain people are authorised to speak to the media, *and no one else*.

If possible, all those who may have to speak to the media should be given some basic training along the lines suggested in this chapter.

Give yourself time to think
Unless the enquiry is a simple one, try to avoid making an instant response. A common technique is to say something like 'I'm sorry but I don't have that information immediately to hand', and promise to phone back. Do sound helpful and positive; ask what information is needed, ask what the journalist's deadline is, and his phone number and/or email address, and say that you'll make sure someone gets back to him in good time.

Always respond within deadlines

We've talked about deadlines already, so you know how important they are to a journalist. Even if for some reason you can't get an answer to the query that's been raised, **you must contact the journalist and say so in good time**. Never leave a tricky enquiry dangling in the air, hoping that the journo will conveniently forget about it. He won't.

Know what you cannot talk about

It is quite usual for organisations to decree that certain subjects are strictly 'out of bounds' when talking to the press. Examples might be corporate financial and legal matters; plans for future developments; manufacturing techniques; competitors' activities. You may want to add others.

Considerable willpower may be needed here! If a journalist phones and asks you if it's true that you are currently negotiating a merger deal with ABC International, or what do you think of Competitor Ltd's recently announced financial results, politely say 'Sorry, but it's our corporate policy never to discuss...' **and stick to that line**, however hard or persistent the questioning gets.

Never say 'No comment'

It's commonly believed that if a journalist asks you a tricky question which you'd rather not answer, you can resolve the situation with a curt 'No comment'. You won't – it's a potential disaster. For example, an editor phones and says he's heard that your company is about to lay off a third of the workforce – is it true? You quickly snap back 'No comment'. **The editor will take this to mean 'it's true'**, and he'll redouble his efforts to get confirmation – by devious means if the story is big enough. If it's not true, say so, clearly and positively. If it *is* true, you should have devised a strategy for dealing with media enquiries before the layoff decision was finalised. (See Chapter 9 for dealing with negative questioning.)

You are never 'off the record'

Once you've said something, it's too late to say 'Oh, by the way, that's off the record'. Once said, it's on the record, like it or not (now you can see the wisdom of engaging the brain before putting the mouth in gear!). If you want to give a journalist a confidential not-to-be-printed or non-attributable background briefing, you must agree that situation very clearly with him *before* you start talking to him.

Be positive, helpful and truthful

Always be polite and pleasant to a journalist; remember, even if you don't like what he's asking you (or the way he's asking it) he's only doing his job. Don't be 'thrown' by aggressive or hostile questioning. And, very importantly, **never tell a journalist a direct lie**. If he uses the false information you've given him and then finds out that it's a lie, he'll never, ever trust you again.

You always represent your organisation

Always stick to the matter in hand and don't get drawn into making personal comments on general matters of the day, politics, sport, etc. If you accidentally make disparaging comments about, say, the performance of the journalist's favourite football team, he may take a dislike to the comments and to you – and that dislike may rub off on your organisation as well. It may sound unreasonable, but that's human nature for you.

Don't ask for special favours

A common beginner's mistake is to ask the editor to give your stories favourable coverage because you advertise in his magazine, or because you've helped him with some market information, or whatever. It won't work, and you've probably irritated someone that you need as a friend. Let your stories stand or fall on their merits.

Finally, always remember the Golden Rule for face-to-face contacts with the press:
If you don't want it to appear in print – DON'T SAY IT.

9

Face to Face – Media Interviews

Now let's move from the general to the particular, and look at the various types of interview situations in which you might find yourself.

There are three basic situations, and you'd be well advised to try to find out which one you're in before you start trying to answer questions.

THE POSITIVE INTERVIEW

This is normally an easy one to handle, and PR-wise it can be quite rewarding. A journalist wants confirmation or more information; you confirm the story and give as much positive information as is relevant and as your press policy permits.

Example 1: You've sent out a news release about a new product. *Question:* 'Does it conform to EU safety legislation?' *Answer:* 'Yes, all our equipment does – and it's been approved by countries like the United States as well.' Nice positive answer – and you've grabbed an opportunity to get in a discreet plug for your export effort!

Example 2: You've been sending out lots of 'order' stories recently. *Question:* 'You seem to be doing well – what's your financial turnover now?' *Answer*: 'Nice of you to say so, and you're right! I'm sorry it's not our policy to talk about actual financial figures, but I can tell you that sales are up by about 30 per cent compared with last year – and the trend's still upward.' You're giving him as factual a statement as you can within corporate media policy guidelines, and subtly prompting further interest about the reasons for this continuing success.

THE DEFENSIVE INTERVIEW
This is the situation where a journalist has got hold of a **negative** story, phones you, and asks you to confirm it and/ or give him more details.

A negative or defensive interview can quickly change from a mildly awkward situation into a PR disaster if it's not handled well. Fortunately for most of us, really defensive interviews are quite rare birds, but be very aware that they can happen and be ready to deal with them smoothly.

Example 1: A journalist phones: 'There's a rumour going around that your company's hit a bad patch and you're going to make a lot of people redundant. Is it true?'

Example 2: Journalist: 'George, my wife was in Tesbury's yesterday looking for your Premier Frozen Fishcakes, and they told her they'd stopped selling them. Has Tesbury's chucked you out?'

Your first reaction to the call is important. If you really and honestly have absolutely no such plans for redundancies, or there's a perfectly good commercial reason why Tesbury's have withdrawn your Premier Fishcakes (like, they're moving upmarket and are going to stock your new Organic SuperFishcakes instead), fine – no problem. Say so (if that's OK with Tesbury's, of course).

However, if you *do* have redundancy plans, or Tesbury's *have* given you the big heave-ho in favour of a competitor, you may experience an instant urge to fudge or delay the issue by saying something like 'Who told you that?' (or worse still, 'That doesn't sound right'), usually said in a somewhat indignant tone of voice. Resist that urge! It will only encourage the journo to think that he's on to something, and he won't reveal his sources to you anyway.

> **At this point, do not confirm or deny a negative story, either directly or indirectly. The key to success in defensive interviews lies in the Boy Scout motto, 'Be Prepared'.**

TRY TO BE PREPARED

If you, as the corporate media contact person, have been forewarned of a possible problem (like the two examples above), you will be able to prepare an answer in advance. *So get all departments primed to contact you as soon as they know of any possible negative situation*, so that you aren't caught on the hop.

However, let's imagine the worst happens – you are taken by surprise. **Don't panic or bluster. Try to gain thinking time**. If appropriate, you might say that you haven't heard about this personally, but you'll look into it right away and get back to him, and what's his phone number and his deadline? Then, as quickly as possible, you get together with everyone concerned in the affair and get all the facts, if you haven't got them already. **Then very carefully prepare and agree a statement, get back to the journalist, read out the statement to him, and stick to it through thick and thin,** no more and no less. 'I'm sorry, but I can't say anything further at this stage' is a useful standby in case of further questioning.

When you have to confirm a negative situation, **always try to make a positive point with it**. This may not be easy, but please do try. For example, if you're having to get rid of people, you may have to confirm some big numbers but try (if appropriate) to emphasise that you'll be relying mainly on natural wastage, and any necessary redundancies will be kept to a minimum, etc.

And finally... Some PR folk have actually been known to try to kill a potentially negative story before it comes out in the press by contacting journalists *and denying it in advance*. Deliberately drawing attention to a negative rumour is like shooting yourself in the foot. Example: 'If you've heard that stupid story going around that we're making lots of people redundant, forget it – it's definitely not true.' After your call a bright journalist will think, 'Well, well, that's interesting. I haven't heard the story, but there's no smoke without fire', so he starts doing a little digging...

THE EXPLORATIVE INTERVIEW

A journalist or features editor phones and asks for some help with a feature, review or article that his publication's putting together. Typically he might want market statistics and/or information about technical developments or market trends in your field.

You've arrived! All those articles designed to make your company an Industry Guru have borne fruit, and it's your big moment. Make the most of it! Here are a few tips:

♦ Find out exactly what information the journo is looking for, because you need to nominate a suitably well-informed (and press-friendly) person in your organisation to talk to him.

♦ Don't sell – **inform**. Banging on about your wonderful product range and what an efficient organisation you are isn't what the journalist wants to hear. He wants **facts**, calmly and authoritatively presented.

♦ If he wants, say, an overview of the market, give him just that. What's happening at the moment? Who's buying what? What are the trends, now and in the foreseeable future? Any sunshine or darkness on the horizon? Then, after the overview, you can seamlessly go on to explain how your organisation's strategy fits into this picture – again, **factually** please.

When your 'expert' is talking to a journalist, said expert may feel that the journalist doesn't seem to understand what he's telling him, obviously knows little or nothing about the subject, and keeps asking the same questions in three different ways. To some experts this can be irritating and frustrating, but **keep cool.** Do not get impatient. Remember – the poor guy's only doing his job, and if he had as much in-depth knowledge about your industry as you do, he wouldn't need to give you this opportunity to get your name in his magazine, would he? Aim to be the 'approachable authority' that's always a pleasure to deal with.

Always bear in mind, when you're talking to a journalist directly or by phone, that this is a great opportunity to project a positive image of your organisation and yourself. By handling media questions in a competent, professional and friendly way, and by appearing as open and honest as possible, your organisation also gains an image of professionalism, openness, friendliness and honesty – and so do you!

10

Face to Face – Holding Effective Press Conferences

Some years ago, press conferences were fashionable because people felt that holding them made their organisation look very important. Companies – and notoriously those in high-tech industries – would call journalists together at the drop of a hat to break some allegedly earth-shattering news. 'Our computers can now compute 10 per cent faster than anyone else's computers.' 'We've just won an important £10,000 government contract in Outer Mongolia.' 'Our offices have been completely refurbished' (a slight exaggeration, this one! But you see what we mean – any excuse to impress the Fourth Estate).

Today, corporate press conferences are not so popular because (a) journalists got fed up with being regularly banged up in a hotel for two or three hours to hear a story which they could have got just as effectively through a press release; and (b) the givers of press conferences began to realise just how expensive they were in terms of executive time, venue hire, catering, drinks, etc., compared with the resultant coverage in the press.

However, having said this, there may still be a place for a very occasional press conference in your media strategy. After all, they do give you a first-class opportunity to meet and greet some of the journalists you've been dealing with on the phone for so long. They also give journos a chance to get to know you and your senior people better, and to gain a more in-depth feel for your organisation.

When to hold a conference

As we've suggested, it needs to be a big or important story whose impact will be maximised by giving journalists the opportunity to ask questions, follow up angles, and write nice big stories. An example might be the announcement of a major corporate merger, takeover or new company formation, and what effect it will have on the market-place. Another would be an important breakthrough in science or technology and its ramifications – e.g. a new form of energy creation, a potential cure for a hitherto virtually incurable disease.

Here's a useful checklist of things to do (and not to do!) once you've decided to hold your first press conference.

Date and time

It is perhaps best to avoid Mondays, which are often editorial conference days for journalists, and maybe Fridays when some like to get home a bit early! Also, remembering that editorial conferences for finalising monthly issues are often around 10th – 15th of the month, it may be as well to avoid that period if you can.

The start time will largely depend on whether you're intending to offer the customary hospitality afterwards (see below). If you are, then allowing say 20 minutes or so for arrival, registration and coffee, maybe an hour for introductions and the presentation(s), followed by up to half an hour for questions, you could invite the journalists for 11.00am with a view to starting luncheon at around 12.45 – 1.00pm.

Venue

Many journalists are based in London or the Home Counties area, so select your venue with this in mind. It needs to be quietly impressive, easily accessible (preferably by public transport) and have good conference and catering facilities adequate for the sort of numbers you'll be inviting. If you can afford it, you won't go far wrong with the tried and trusted 'central London hotel' solution.

Avoid the temptation to go for a way-out venue which you're sure the press will find really exciting and memorable – it can backfire on you. A company once held a press conference on a Thames pleasure barge which, after the journalists came aboard, weighed anchor and chugged off on a non-stop return journey to Tilbury or somewhere. Unfortunately several journalists were pushed for time and wanted to get back to their offices immediately after questions were finished, but were forced to hang around in mid-stream for another couple of hours while pre-lunch drinks and lunch were consumed before the barge moored up again back at the start point. The only escape route would have been to swim ashore; no one took it ...

Invitations

Write a warmly-worded, friendly letter of invitation, which should be personally addressed to each journalist you intend to invite. There should be a heading that summarises what the event is about, plus the date, the time, and the venue. The body of the letter will give just enough information to grab the journalists' interest, but won't give the whole story away. It is also as well to include a small form for a response: 'I will/will not be able to attend the press conference'. Focus particularly on your 'hit list' of priority publications that you use in your features work, and make a special effort to get someone to come from each of them.

If possible, send out the letter at least three or four weeks before the date of the conference; journalists' diaries fill up quite a lot in advance. Then, about ten days before the conference, get on the phone and follow up those you haven't heard from. Don't forget to notify the venue of the numbers 24 hours before the event.

Press packs

These are essential. For each journalist you'll need a reasonably smart folder (personalised with the journo's name is a nice touch) containing a press release giving them the story to save them work, pics where appropriate, a backgrounder on the product(s) or organisations involved in the story, and a profile of your own organisation. You should also have a pin-on name badge for each guest, which you affix as they arrive and sign in. However, we suggest that you do *not* hand the press packs out when the journalists first arrive – some of them may take the pack and quietly bunk off without listening to the presentations. Leave the packs out of sight until after question time.

Speakers

Who you pick to make the presentation(s) will naturally depend on the subject. However, do try to put senior people up in front of the journalists; it subtly emphasises the importance of the event if, for example, the journos are welcomed by your MD or general manager and then introduced to the R&D and marketing directors to make the presentations.

Needless to say, all your people at the press conference must be briefed with the points in Chapter 8 that we listed earlier. It's all too easy (and sharp journalists know this!) to relax one's guard a little too far after a pleasant buffet lunch and a glass or two of the venue's house white, and say something it would have been better to have left unsaid. Remember the corporate disaster that resulted from the chairman of a certain retail chain cheerfully describing some of his products as 'crap' at a press conference!

Refreshments

You could offer morning coffee when they arrive to sign in, and after presentations and questions – if you're feeling expansive but not expensive – a choice of house wine or soft drinks with a fairly simple but well-prepared and presented buffet lunch. Don't forget possible vegetarians. And even if you are feeling expensive, don't overdo the hospitality with a three-course lunch accompanied by vintage claret, brandy and port. Not many will really appreciate it, and it could be teatime before you've got rid of the last of the stragglers.

Afterwards

After the conference, send copies of the press release and background material a.s.a.p. to all the journos on your normal distribution list that you didn't invite, or who couldn't make it. It's also a good plan to hold a post-mortem with your colleagues who were at the conference to see whether any of them were asked questions during lunch, or if any of the journos showed a particular interest which would repay following up.

(11)

And if They Get it Wrong . . .

The great majority of journalists and editors are very conscientious about getting their stories right. However, they are human beings and so, very occasionally, they may Get It Wrong. Where do you stand if, for example, a magazine or newspaper publishes what you feel is a libellous statement about your organisation or a member of it? Or writes something that you believe to be untrue and/or damaging and/or capable of bringing you into disrepute?

The good news is that this will probably never happen to you. Most organisations, even those regularly active in press relations, will never be affected by a serious media cock-up. But in case you ever become one of the unlucky minority, here are some useful guidelines.

Move quickly

If you feel it necessary to take some sort of action, whatever it may be, start moving as soon as the offending piece comes to your notice. Whatever action is deemed appropriate, it will be all the more impressive and effective with all concerned if you're fast off the starting blocks.

Think before you act

Just how bad is this incident? It's very easy to get worked up into a steaming froth of indignation – or get provoked into one by colleagues who scent excitement, but who aren't responsible for subsequent relationships with the press! Indeed, your first instinct may be to send for m'Learned Friends and, as a very last resort, recourse to law may become necessary.

However, before you get fired up and start serving writs, it's worthwhile considering that going to law can be very expensive, and may not prove all that advantageous in the long run. Libel cases, for example, are notoriously tricky; you might win, but also you might lose. Most publishing companies carry insurance against actions for libel, damages, etc., but if you lose you may end up having to pay your own costs – and possibly theirs, too. The Learned Friends will usually make sure that this adds up to some big, big figures. Also, the resultant publicity won't do anything for the future take-up of your stories by other publications, who may see your organisation as a keen litigant that's best avoided.

Negotiate first

For these reasons, **always start by negotiating**. There are *degrees* of getting things wrong, of course, and these will help to determine the course of the negotiation.

For example, if there has obviously been a straightforward misunderstanding, or even an unfortunate typographical error, suing everyone in sight clearly isn't the best way forward. Instead, phone the editor. Calmly point out that there seems to be an error in his latest issue, and quote chapter and verse. You're not going to throw a hissy fit over this, but could something perhaps be done to put things right? How about some positive editorial in his next issue to counterbalance it? And, er, it just so happens that we are even now writing a really interesting article about . . .

We've used this method with some success. But even if the offence is a lot more serious than a misunderstanding or a misprint, don't deploy the Weapons of Mass Destruction just yet – there are still diplomatic options to explore.

GETTING AN APOLOGY PRINTED

In a more serious situation, it will be a good plan to begin by having a quick word with a lawyer, preferably one with experience in this area. Fax or email a copy of the offending piece, and ask for an initial opinion. In law, is this libellous? Defamatory? Damaging? Do you, or could you, have a reasonable case if it came to court?

Then, even if your brief reckons it's a borderline case, contact the editor. The alleged damaging statement, or whatever, has been aired in public so your objective will be the publication of a retraction and an unqualified apology. Ideally this should:

◆ appear in the next issue of the publication

◆ be printed on the same page as the offending item

◆ occupy the same amount of space on the page.

You should also ask for the right to agree the wording of the retraction in advance.

You will now almost certainly encounter stout resistance, because *most editors have a deep-seated aversion to publishing apologies.* Well, let's face it – would *you* like to have to tell all your loyal readers that your magazine sometimes gets it badly wrong? So the editor's first reaction may be to try to dismiss the idea. 'Oh come on, a retraction's going a bit far, surely it wasn't as bad as all that? I can't see there's really anything to apologise for,' and so on. You then counter this by detailing, politely but formally, the actual damage that the magazine's action has caused, or could cause, you or your organisation. If you can back this with hard facts, a favourable legal opinion and a reasonable (but firm) attitude, you may get the editor – albeit reluctantly! – to change his mind.

Here's an actual example of a serious nasty. Naturally we've made it suitably anonymous!

Demanding an apology – an example
Once upon a time, there was a computer systems

manufacturer who secured a large and very valuable order from a prominent building society. The manufacturer's PR agency distributed (with the building society's full approval and cooperation) a press release announcing the order, complete with a suitably captioned pic showing the society's general manager sitting at a desk signing the contract whilst surrounded by various executives from both organisations – a very common practice. Good bona fide order story, good take-up by most of the trade press.

However, one magazine decided to play it differently. It didn't use the order story, but it did use the pic of the signing ceremony (without caption or acknowledgement) as part of a 'fun' competition inviting readers to guess what the man sitting at the desk was saying. Unfortunately the magazine also described him as 'the character looking like a rather shady second-hand car salesman', or words to that effect.

The building society's general manager was a well-known and respected figure in the financial world. Incandescent with rage, he issued an ultimatum. He would cancel the entire order unless the magazine published a full and unreserved apology – and he left it up to the computer manufacturer to arrange it. Pretty unfair on the manufacturer, you might think – but who argues with a customer armed with a million quid or so?

Within hours the manufacturer's PR agency had consulted a lawyer, got a positive opinion, contacted the editor concerned, and firmly insisted on the necessary apology. The editor's initial reaction was to refuse, on the grounds that the agency had sent him the pic without any stipulations about how it should be used, and anyway, it was only a bit of fun, wasn't it? The agency pointed out that (a) the pic was captioned and attached to the press release, so it was clearly provided as an integral part of the order story – hence the magazine had used it for a purpose for which it was never intended; (b) the magazine's unfortunate description of the very respectable general manager had brought him into ridicule and contempt; and (c) the computer manufacturer would hold the publishers and the editor fully responsible for the loss of profit that would result if the very large order were cancelled. It was made clear that a claim would be pursued through the courts if no apology were forthcoming.

The result was a retraction and apology in the magazine's next issue, with wording agreed in advance by the building society's general manager. It appeared on the same page as the offending 'competition' had done, and took up the same amount of space. The order was saved, and the PR agency removed the offending magazine from its distribution list for future releases – just in case.

As Sir Winston Churchill once said: 'To jaw-jaw is better than to war-war'!

Press Relations Case Study 1 – the Unknown Alpha

This case study won't provoke 'Wow!' and whistles of surprise, but we've included it because it describes the benefits gained from the first press release ever issued by a very small company. Because the company was small and completely unknown to the press, it would normally have taken several releases before it achieved editorial take-up. However, connecting it to a universally-known name meant that the release produced positive results first time. And 'The Case of the Unknown Alpha' shows how a good story can still do sterling service as a marketing tool long after it has appeared in the press.

Alpha Health and Safety Ltd, formed in 1995 by a bright and highly qualified guy called Jim Collins, specialises in industrial health and safety consultancy and planning and monitoring to official CDM (Construction Design and Management) requirements on construction sites. Alpha is unashamedly small; it's basically Jim and his PA, bringing in specialist outside help as and when needed.

We first met Jim at a local business club breakfast meeting shortly after he had completed a big, big CDM job for

Weetabix, the well-known breakfast cereal maker. He told us just how big the job was, and for an outfit of Alpha's size it sounded highly impressive.

With our curiosity for a good story alerted, we dug a bit further. It turned out that, thanks to Alpha, the Weetabix project achieved what must have been one of the lowest accident rates ever seen on a job of this type and size. Although Jim wasn't a client of ours, and had never done any PR-type stuff before, we persuaded him to 'have a go' on the strength of the story and, in particular, the strength of his client Weetabix, a household name known to every editor and journalist in the country.

Would Weetabix play ball? We contacted the person who had been in charge of the project. As we expected, the company had very strict rules concerning the publicising of information. We couldn't name any of their people, use any attributable comments or name any of their departments, and the release would be closely vetted at high level. Did we still want to go ahead? Yes, we did – and the final Weetabix-approved version is shown below. (We must have done something right, because Weetabix only made four very slight amendments to our original draft!)

The release was taken up by several publications in the construction industry and the local press. As a direct result of that story Alpha won another contract, this time to carry out dust monitoring in a dockside silo in East Anglia – not so large, but certainly well worth the cost of writing and sending out the press release.

Another useful side-effect of the Weetabix story was that some of Alpha's previous clients read it and phoned to comment on it; as Jim Collins says, it helped him to maintain some valued contacts. And even now, two years later, the impact of that release isn't finished by a long chalk. Jim reckons that the same impressive story is still helping Alpha to get contracts, because he always includes copies of it as part of the company's corporate profile that he submits with construction contract bids.

The Unknown Alpha – the Press release

Weetabix AP2 construction project 'twice as safe as national average'

The rate of industrial accidents sustained during a major CDM civil engineering project for Weetabix Ltd in Northamptonshire must be among the lowest ever recorded on a project of this size, according to site safety planning supervisors Alpha Health and Safety Ltd. There was just one reportable accident during 480,000 man-hours worked by the 200 construction employees on the site, representing 0.5 accidents per 100 employees – well under the construction industry's national average of 1.2 accidents per 100 in 2001, as published by the Health and Safety Executive.

The Weetabix project, known as AP2, involved 46 separate contracting companies, up to 200 workers on site each day, and 35 cranes were used at various times during the project. Phase One of AP2 included the complete refurbishment of an old five-storey mill building and another large single-storey building. Site access was hampered by a nearby road, river and railway line, and part of the work had to be carried out in freezing cold, wet and windy conditions. Normal production also had to be maintained in buildings adjacent to the construction site. Phase Two covered the installation of plant and equipment to manufacture Weetabix's new 'Minibix' product.

Weetabix appointed Alpha Health and Safety to carry out all safety planning, co-ordination and monitoring for AP2. With the number of employees involved, together with the physical restrictions of the site, strict safety procedures were essential. Alpha's managing director, Jim Collins, explains: 'We checked the health and safety systems of all the 46 contractors involved, ran more than 1,700 site safety induction sessions, issued over 3,000 safe working permits, held regular site safety meetings, and provided a full-time safety co-ordinator on site for the duration of the contract.'

'The result of our efforts was very gratifying,' Collins continued. 'We only had the one reportable accident, when someone slipped on a stair which led to a three-day absence from work.'

Established in 1932, Weetabix Limited is the leading British breakfast cereal manufacturer with brands including Weetabix, Alpen and Ready Brek. The company is headquartered at an 85-acre site in Burton Latimer, Northamptonshire, with a further two factories at Corby. The company currently produces more than 70 million breakfast biscuits a week, and exports its products to over 80 countries worldwide.

Alpha Health and Safety Limited, based in Corby, Northamptonshire, specialises in industrial health and safety consultancy, and planning and monitoring to CDM requirements for major construction sites. Since May 1995 the company has acted as safety advisor and planning supervisor on more than 165 CDM-notifiable projects, during which time it has recorded only three reportable accidents, the most serious being a fractured wrist.

Alpha Health and Safety was formed by its present managing director, Jim Collins, who is a Member of the Institutes of Industrial Engineers and Occupational Safety and Health, a Fellow of the Royal Society of Health, and a Member of the Association of Planning Supervisors.

-ends-

Release issued: 5th February 2002
For more information, please contact:
Jim Collins, Alpha Health and Safety Ltd, Tel: 01234 567891 Fax: 01234 567892 Email: info:address.co.uk

Press Relations Case Study 2 – Albert the Wonderloo

This case study shows how the imaginative use of a story not only brought in positive enquiries, but also prompted the start of a whole new line of business. It illustrates the benefits you can gain from developing a 'feel' for a good story, and the value of publishing your press releases on the news page of your corporate website.

Fenland Hydrotech Ltd, a client of the authors' press relations agency, is an independent firm of consulting engineers with expertise in water engineering projects such as pipelines, sewerage, storm drainage and effluent treatment.

Fenland's managing director, Stephen Winpenny, bought an old barn in the Yorkshire Dales and converted it into a holiday cottage. One day he was talking to Pam about this and happened to mention that, because the barn had been built on rock and couldn't have a septic tank or connection to a main sewer, he'd devised a unique purpose-made individual sewage treatment system for it, based on 'green' principles.

Stephen, who saw the project as just one of those sorts of things that Fenland folk were doing all the time, had privately nicknamed it 'Albert' ('the Wonderloo' bit was ours). He hadn't thought of Albert as newsworthy, but Pam's feel for a story told her that this one could be a goer. Her thinking ran like this: (1) other people must come up against similar problems in various parts of this country and in the wider world, so there could be interest among second-home buyers, developers, builders, plumbers, and so on; (2) Albert's 'green' technology – fully aerobic, non-chemical, environmentally friendly, odour-free and cheap to operate – was new, unique and clever; and (3) the Wonderloo would provide a good example of Fenland's ability to solve difficult hydrological problems for its clients, which was one of the main strategic objectives of the press campaign.

We did see one possible problem. The story could lose impact if we told it exactly as it happened – a clever engineer designing a sewage treatment system for his own holiday cottage. So we took a slight liberty with the actuality and wrote it up as a development project carried out by Fenland Hydrotech for an anonymous 'customer'. This, as you will immediately have noticed, ran counter to our advice not to raise unanswered questions in news stories, because the obvious possible query was: 'Who *was* the customer?' We discussed it and decided that the risk of someone asking the question was quite small, and worth taking for a good story. And if push came to shove, we could reasonably put our tongues in our cheeks and say that the customer didn't want his name to be used (well, we wouldn't really be telling a lie, now, would we?).

Take a look at the release that went out (page 108). You might try to fault it on the grounds that it was over-long, that it went into too much technical detail about the sewage treatment process involved. But remember, the overall aim of the press campaign strategy was to create an image of Fenland as a clever, innovative organisation in the hydrological engineering business; hence the need to give it a lavish helping of sewage disposal technology. We just had to hope that editors didn't read it while they were munching their lunchtime sarnies.

Pam's instinct was right. The Albert release was used by several magazines, and a goodly number of enquiries were received from readers including house-builders, architects, local authorities and building industry reference libraries. Two of the magazines operated a reader reply service, and these two alone brought in more than 50 enquiries. Readers in Ireland showed considerable interest, as new and stricter laws regarding sewage disposal had recently been passed in the Republic.

Fenland's comprehensive website includes a news page carrying copies of articles and press releases, and the Albert release was duly added to it. Many months later – long after the magazine stories had been forgotten – the release on the website was still producing a steady trickle of one or two enquiries a month. One of these ex-web enquiries resulted in a project in Lincolnshire to provide specifications and advisory services, but virtually all the other enquiries were for the supply and installation of individual Wonderloos rather than consultancy.

This started Fenland thinking. They were consulting engineers, but if there was a viable market for making and supplying Alberts, why not take advantage of it? So Steve Winpenny took his brainchild, looked at it after two years' personal experience, decided on some technical enhancements, and – as we write this – he is prototyping an updated design and is planning to go into production with it shortly, in partnership with the firm that built and installed the original Albert up in the Yorkshire Dales.

And to think that the world would never have known about the unique 'green' technology and the other benefits of Albert the Wonderloo (and Fenland wouldn't have had its new business opportunity) if Pam hadn't spotted the story's press potential in the first place.

Albert the Wonderloo – the press release

Fenland develops unique non-chemical sewage treatment system for individual premises

Fenland Hydrotech Ltd, a firm of consulting engineers specialising in water engineering, has developed a new and unique solution to the problem of sewage treatment at premises that cannot be connected to main sewerage networks or septic tanks. The system is fully aerobic, non-chemical, environmentally friendly and odour-free; it takes up less space than similar systems, can be installed above or below ground, and requires minimal maintenance.

Fenland developed the system to solve a problem posed by a customer who had purchased a cottage converted from an old commercial building, built on rock and with no connections to a main sewer. It employs the technology used in large urban sewage treatment systems and applies it on a small scale, mixing incoming waste products with activated sludge and using a continuous stream of air bubbles to agitate the mix and keep bacteria constantly moving. Traditional systems working on the mechanical Rotating Biological Contactor (RBC) principle can allow anaerobic bacteria to breed in the inlet section of the plant, causing unpleasant odours which must be vented into the environment. As the customer's cottage is very close to other buildings, this would have been unacceptable; the Fenland system's continuous oxygenation process eliminated the problem as it is virtually odour-free.

When the contents of the receiving tank have been broken down by biological action the mixture moves into a settlement tank, where the activated sludge settles to the bottom. Clean water rises to the top of the settlement tank and is removed to an outside drain, and the activated sludge is pumped back into the receiving tank.

Fenland Hydrotech managing director Stephen Winpenny says that the unit has been operating trouble-free for 18 months. 'It has coped perfectly well with excreta, toilet tissues and biological kitchen waste such as potato peelings, and the electricity required to run its aerator and pump has cost no more than a light bulb,' he claims. 'We can now confidently offer this solution to anyone who, for whatever reason, cannot connect to a main sewer or install a septic tank.'

The unit in this instance was installed above ground and measures only 6ft x 6ft x 2ft, compared with typical RBC systems' 8ft x 4ft x 4ft. It complies with relevant Environment Agency requirements and building regulations and is fully automatic and quiet in operation; its aerator works continuously, and a timer activates the pump for a few minutes every couple of hours.

For commercial enquiries about the system, please contact Fenland on 01832 734612.

Fenland Hydrotech Limited, based in Thrapston, Northamptonshire, is an independent firm of consulting engineers providing professional services to public and private sector clients in the UK and overseas. The company has particular expertise in the area of water engineering, including pipelines, sewerage, storm drainage, tunnelling, water treatment and distribution, and effluent treatment.

Fenland Hydrotech is a member of the Association of Consulting Engineers, and its Quality Assurance system is accredited to ISO 9001/BS5750 part 1. It provides a complete project management service from initial appraisal, through detailed design and documentation to contract administration, site supervision and cost control.

-ends-

Release issued: 18th June 2002
For illustration, colour pic of premises, or more information, contact:
Pam Austin, Editorial Services, Tel: 01858 535466 Fax: 01858 535484
Email: pam@editorialservices.co.uk

Press Relations Case Study 3 – lastminutesermon.com

This last one's an absolute cracker! It's one of those once-in-a-lifetime happenings which certainly isn't typical of the results you could normally expect from your average press release. However, it provides a good example of the need to be ready for the unexpected in case it does happen, and it illustrates some actual 'face-to-face' situations and how they were handled.

As well as being in the press relations business the authors of this book, Pam and Bob Austin, are active members of their local C of E church – Pam is a churchwarden, and Bob is a Reader (a lay minister who leads worship, preaches and teaches). During Bob's Readership he has researched, written and delivered more than 250 sermons, which several different local congregations seem to have appreciated.

One day, Pam had a bright idea. Why not offer these sermons – which had been written and preached by a professional writer and authorised minister – to busy ministers and teachers, who sometimes find it difficult to find time to write their own sermons or prepare school assemblies? Because such situations often arise at the last minute a fast-response service would be needed, and the answer was to offer the sermons on-line from a well-designed and user-friendly website. From this thinking emerged a website called 'lastminutesermon.com', initially offering a selection of 50 + sermons, and a choice of payment and despatch methods.

The site was scheduled go live on 30th March 2003, just before Palm Sunday (the Sunday before Easter), and to provide a flavour of the churchmanship, etc. of the sermons we offered site visitors a free sample sermon suitable for Palm Sunday. To publicise the new website we wrote a straightforward press release (copy below) aimed at all the mainstream religious journals in the UK, together with religious correspondents on the main national newspapers.

What we hadn't allowed for was the possibility that George Bush and Tony Blair would start a war in Iraq, carefully timed to clash with our launch. With the entire UK media apparently totally absorbed by war news as our launch date approached, what chance would our website have? However, we decided that we had to go ahead with the timing as planned because we felt it was very important to try to have some publicity in place before Easter Sunday (20th April).

Before the launch we did a final brainstorming session to uncover any obvious face-to-face negatives, and came up with some possible questions along the lines of 'Shouldn't ministers write their own sermons?', 'Are you suggesting that some clergy can't write sermons?', and 'Can it be right to make a profit from selling the Word of God?'

We agreed in advance how we would deal with them if they came up. For example, the question about ministers writing their own sermons: 'In an ideal world, yes – but the world isn't always an ideal place for increasingly busy clergy. The reality is that many vicars in rural areas now have to look after not one church and community, as they would have in years gone by, but maybe five or six – that means less and less time to prepare sermons.' Questions about the ability of clergy to write sermons: 'No one can be good at everything, but this isn't so much a question of ability as of workload and priorities. If you have to choose between handling an urgent pastoral problem and writing a sermon, which do you do? We can help to resolve that problem.' And for those querying the morality of making money from the Word of God: 'If you go into a bookshop for a Bible, you wouldn't expect to get it free. And professional ministers do get paid for what they do.' All good, positive answers.

The press release was mailed out on the same day that the website went live, and we waited to see what would happen. Two days later, the story was covered by the *Guardian* newspaper, who weighed in with a touch of humour and some good positive comments: 'Homily just a click away for clergy...each a listener-friendly 10 minutes long...free from fundamentalist ranting and trendy liberalism', etc. Nice one, we thought.

'Nice' was an understatement for what happened next! The *Guardian* piece was like a small earth tremor that starts a major avalanche. From then on, the telephone hardly stopped ringing – it seemed as if the press, radio and TV were having a feeding frenzy over our harmless little story. Some of the coverage we know that we gained:

Press: *The Times, Daily Telegraph,* the *Observer,* the *Church Times* (two pieces a week apart – the first saying that they thought it was an April Fool's Day joke until they checked out the website!), the *Scottish Sun,* and our local newspapers such as the *Northampton Chronicle and Echo.* We were also contacted by the Press Association. Overseas, the story was used by newspapers and magazines in the USA, Germany, Sweden and Argentina.

Radio: The BBC put the story on its Internet news page. This was followed by interviews with the *Today* programme on BBC Radio 4, and with local BBC radio stations including Cambridge, Southern Counties, Humberside, West Midlands, Northampton, Leicester, Hereford and Worcester, Bristol, Leeds, Jersey, and a local independent station – Hereward FM. We also did live interviews with Irish Radio, and two American chat shows – Westwood One Radio in Washington, DC and the Randy Miller Show in Kansas City.

Television: Anglia TV came and filmed our village and local church, and interviewed us. They ran the item one evening in their 6.00pm news programme. Another local TV programme, BBC *East Midlands Today,* did something similar except that their item also included a reading from lastminutesermon's Palm Sunday sermon.

Even for experienced professionals like us, the sheer volume of interest and range of questions was daunting. However, it proved the value of our pre-launch brain-storming session. For example, the first question Bob was asked by the formidable John Humphrys on the BBC's *Today* programme was a belligerent 'Shouldn't vicars write their own sermons – it's cheating if they use someone else's, isn't it?' As an opener it could easily have thrown Bob if he hadn't been prepared for it.

Another point that came out of the exercise was the maxim 'think before you speak' – that anything you say to a journalist may appear in print. During a telephone interview with a journalist from the *Church Times*, Bob was asked whether the website wasn't really an oblique criticism of the general standard of clergy sermons. 'No,' he said, mentally searching for the right phrase, 'we didn't intend to cock a snook at the clergy.' In the cold light of post-interview, Bob wished he hadn't use the rather ugly expression 'cock a snook' – but he had, and, of course, that's just what the *Church Times* printed! Not exactly damaging, but it could certainly have been put more elegantly.

Interestingly, however, we also found that a memorable phrase would stick and do the rounds – in this case, Bob's inspired description of the sermons as 'pulpit-tested' in an early radio interview. This expression was subsequently used by several other interviewers who'd heard it used on the earlier interview.

The result of our press release was a flood of free – and almost entirely positive – publicity in the UK and overseas worth literally hundreds of thousands of pounds. The publicity prompted visits to the lastminute-sermon.com site by some 14,000 people during the first three weeks after its launch.

What was it about this apparently innocent little product launch that grabbed so much media attention, smack in the middle of the war in Iraq? After all, buying ready-made sermons and homilies individually or in books has been going on (albeit in a fairly small way) for literally hundreds of years. All we had done was to put ours on the Internet and send out a bog-standard format news release about it.

We guess that there were several reasons why the media saw this as a 'good' story. One was the whole idea of spreading the Word of God via the Internet – an unusual and perhaps intriguing combination of religion and modern technology. Then we quickly realised that none of the interviewers seemed to know that some preachers already bought sermons, so there was a sort of shock-horror 'Well, I never heard of such a thing!' factor involved. And it's also possible that the media saw the rather quaint story as a welcome relief in a news environment dominated by the horror, bitterness and recriminations of the war in Iraq.

And who knows? Maybe the professional formatting and writing style of the press release had something to do with it, too...

lastminutesermon.com – the press release

New buy-on-line sermon library
Professionally-written Christian sermons for ministers and teachers
Topical free sample sermon for Palm Sunday

Newly-launched **lastminutesermon.com**, a unique buy-on-line service for busy Christian ministers and teachers, offers carefully-crafted sermons all based on Biblical texts and themes. Using **lastminutesermons**, ministers and teachers from a variety of Christian traditions can now deliver thoroughly researched and topical sermons at short notice, or facilitate study, youth and activity groups and devise informal services or school assemblies using the sermons as building blocks.

To celebrate its launch, **lastminutesermon.com** is offering a typical – and topical – free sample sermon suitable for Palm Sunday.

Sermons, including the free Palm Sunday sermon, can be quickly and easily downloaded from the **lastminutesermon.com** website. **lastminutesermons** are thought-provoking, inspirational and educational, and do not involve extremism or doctrinally controversial views. They are listed on the website by textual references and by theme title; each one costs only £8.00, payable by Credit or Direct Debit card or by cheque. **lastminutesermon.com** tithes five per cent of all sermon income to charitable causes.

lastminutesermons have all been written and preached by Bob Austin, a professional writer and Benedictine novice oblate who is also a Church of England Reader, licensed to preach, teach and lead worship in the Diocese of Peterborough. 'In spite of received wisdom to the contrary, there's a hunger among congregations for an element of teaching in sermons,' he says. 'Setting the biblical scene in the context of beliefs, traditions and customs in 1st Century Palestine has become a "must". People often ask me why no-one has explained things like that to them before, and they say that it makes it so much easier to understand.'

Currently the **lastminutesermon.com** site lists just over 50 sermons covering a wide range of texts and themes. Further sermons are regularly being transcribed from notes and added to the buy-on-line collection. If a minister or teacher needs a sermon on a theme not currently listed, they are encouraged to contact **lastminutesermon.com** to enquire if one may be available on the text or theme they require.

-ends-

Release issued: 30th March 2003
lastminutesermon website address: www.lastminutesermon.com
Editors requiring more information, please contact:
Bob or Pam Austin, Tel: 01858 535466 Fax: 01858 535484
E-mail: bob@lastminutesermon.com

Index